Josie Mpama/Palmer

OHIO SHORT HISTORIES OF AFRICA

This series of Ohio Short Histories of Africa is meant for those who are looking for a brief but lively introduction to a wide range of topics in African history, politics, and biography, written by some of the leading experts in their fields.

Josie Mpama/Palmer

Get Up and Get Moving

Robert R. Edgar

OHIO UNIVERSITY PRESS

ATHENS

Ohio University Press, Athens, Ohio 45701
ohioswallow.com
© 2020 by Ohio University Press
All rights reserved

Printed in the United States of America
Ohio University Press books are printed on acid-free paper ⊗ ™

30 29 28 27 26 25 24 23 22 21 20   5 4 3 2 1

Library of Congress Cataloging-in-Publication Data

Names: Edgar, Robert R., author.
Title: Josie Mpama/Palmer : get up and get moving / Robert R. Edgar.
Other titles: Ohio short histories of Africa.
Description: Athens, Ohio : Ohio University Press, 2020. | Series: Ohio
   short histories of Africa | Includes bibliographical references and
   index.
Identifiers: LCCN 2020001392 | ISBN 9780821424100 (paperback)
   | ISBN
   9780821440940 (pdf)
Subjects: LCSH: Mpama, Josie, 1903-1979. | Women political
   activists--South
   Africa--Biography. | Communists--South Africa--Biography. |
   Anti-apartheid activists--South Africa--Biography. | South
   Africa--History--20th century.
Classification: LCC DT1927.M63 E34 2020 | DDC 968.05092--dc23
LC record available at https://lccn.loc.gov/2020001392

*To the memory of Comrade Professor Phil Bonner,
a friend who understood the distinction between
scholarship and activism as well as how
they can enrich each other*

Contents

Illustrations

Preface

Researching the Life of Josie Mpama/Palmer

Piecing together the life of Josie Mpama/Palmer was challenging and required me to draw on a range of oral and written sources. My initial interest in her emanated from my research on Edwin Thabo Mofutsanyana, her common-law husband from the late 1920s to the late 1930s. I interviewed him at length in Lesotho (where he lived in exile) in the 1980s. After the dramatic change in South Africa's political environment in 1990, I started collecting information on Josie. A starting point was an interview that Julia Wells conducted with her in 1977 that focused on her activism in the South African city of Potchefstroom. I interviewed two of her daughters, Carol and Hilda, in 1995 as well as close friends who lived in her neighborhood in 1998. Later I interviewed four of her grandchildren, Belinda and Virginia Palmer and Lorraine and Bella Johnson, who spent much time in her home in Mzimhlophe when they were growing up and who gave me their generation's perspective on her.

I also identified a variety of written sources. I combed through Communist Party of South Africa (CPSA), left-of-center, and black newspapers published in the 1930s and 1940s. These contained materials on her public activities as well as columns by her on women's issues.

Government records at the National Archives in Pretoria yielded information on her father, Stephen Mpama: a divorce case, a criminal trial, and the estate record at his death. The archives also contained extensive Potchefstroom municipal records on the protests of the late 1920s in which Josie Mpama participated. In the 1920s and 1930s, the Justice Department issued regular reports on communist activities in the Union of South Africa that occasionally mentioned her activities. I also consulted the Justice Department's banning file on Josie Mpama from the 1940s and 1950s.

Critical records came from the papers of two important figures in the CPSA, Jack and Ray Simons, held at the University of Cape Town. Their papers include minutes of a critical CPSA central committee meeting at the end of 1938.

A crucial breakthrough came in 1998 when I examined the extensive Communist International (Comintern) and CPSA records at the Russian State Archive of Socio-Political History in Moscow. The CPSA may have been careful about defining its image to outsiders, but its records are remarkably revealing and do not shy away from revealing internal splits, personal disputes, and ideological controversies. When Josie was in Moscow for party training in 1935, she left writings, including an autobiography about her youth and candid essays detailing her views on CPSA matters. While there, she testified at an important Comintern hearing on ideological disputes within the CPSA that featured Moses Kotane and Lazar Bach.

Despite consulting this range of sources, I still found significant gaps in reconstructing phases of Josie's life. I hope that other historians will unearth more material.

A Note on the Names Mpama and Palmer

Josie used two surnames, Mpama and Palmer. Mpama (sometimes spelled "M'Pama") came from her father, Stephen Mpama. The change to Palmer, an anglicization of Mpama, came in the mid-1930s when she and her family were living in Sophiatown. The advantage of taking the name Palmer is that her children could, with a European name, qualify for better schools. Because she shifted back and forth between the names throughout her life, I have avoided confusion by often referring to her simply as Josie in my narrative.

Acknowledgments

Research for this book was assisted by grants from the Fulbright Program in 1995 that afforded me the opportunity to begin researching Josie Mpama in South Africa and from the International Research and Exchanges Board that allowed me to travel to Moscow for several weeks in 1998. Apollon Davidson facilitated my stay in Moscow, and his colleague Valentin Gorodnov walked me through the bureaucratic labyrinth to arrange for research permits and assisted in identifying relevant files at the Russian Center for the Preservation and Study of Contemporary History. They were generous hosts, and I cannot thank them enough for their support. Dan Johns arranged accommodation for me in Moscow and has been a constant source of encouragement.

I have benefited enormously from the comments of Julie Wells, Noor Nieftagodien, Iris Berger, Helen Hopps, Andre Odendaal, Elinor Sisulu, Russell Martin, and several anonymous reviewers of earlier versions of my manuscript. The remarkable Africana bibliographer and historian Peter Limb alerted me to several newspaper columns mentioning Stephen Mpama.

Librarians and archivists have been instrumental in identifying sources. Michelle Pickover and Gabriele Mohale of the Historical Papers Archive at Witwatersrand University and Najwa Hendrickse of the Cape Town campus of the National Library of South Africa have been especially helpful.

As I was conceptualizing this study, I profited from a seminar organized by Phil Bonner and Noor Nieftagodien at the Local History project at Witwatersrand University.

Sally Gaulle assisted me with preserving photographs from a Palmer family album. I thank her for her friendship and dedication to my project. Rita Potenza assisted with identifying additional photographic material.

I benefited from the cooperation and support of Josie Palmer's children, grandchildren, and great-grandchildren: Hilda Johnson, Francis Palmer, Carol Matsie, Lorraine Johnson, Bella Johnson, Belinda Palmer, Virginia Palmer, and Nicolai Allard.

Vusi Khumalo arranged for an interview with Lorraine Johnson.

I continue to rely on the support of the Department of African Studies at Howard University and the Department of Historical Studies at Stellenbosch University.

Throughout my professional life, I have enjoyed the support of a network of friends who have encouraged my research. I would like to thank Albert and Anna Mari Grundlingh, Gail Gerhart, Peter Limb, Brenda

Randolph, Chris and Pam Saunders, David Ambrose, Robert Vinson, Anne Mager, Charles and Eileen Villa Vicencio, Sally Gaule, May McClain, Charlotte and Pioneer Nhlapo, Mbye Cham, Sehoai Santho, Motlatsi Thabane, Hilary Sapire, David and Manana Coplan, Mathews and Pinky Phosa, Tito Mboweni, Roger and Hilary Southall, Luyanda Msumza, Vangi Titi, Neo and Khabo Ramoupi, Tshepo Moloi, Bruce Murray, Anthea Josias, David Wallace, Trish and Greg Josias, Andre Odendaal, Zohra Ibrahim, Rehana Odendaal, Adam Odendaal, Nadia Odendaal, David and Polly Dean, and Ben Carton and his *impi*.

I salute the League of Extraordinary Gentlemen for managing to publish dozens of books without once using the word *zombie* in a title.

As always, I thank my son Leteane for beginning and ending every day with a smile.

Finally, I would like to express my appreciation of Gill Berchowitz of Ohio University Press, who has guided several of my publications to fruition. She has been a mentor whose vision has contributed to not only past and present generations of Africanists but also to the next one.

Introduction

An Untidy Hero

"We women are the backbone of the nation," declared Josie Mpama/Palmer, whose life as a political activist in South Africa was a testament to her assertion.[1] From leading a major protest against lodger's permits in Potchefstroom in the late 1920s to promoting community struggles on the Witwatersrand in the 1930s and 1940s and from playing a leading role in antipass campaigns in the 1940s and 1950s to being one of the founders of the Federation of South African Women (FEDSAW) in 1954, she was a pillar of the freedom struggle. Thus, it was fitting that in June 2004, the South African government recognized her service to the nation by posthumously awarding her the Order of Luthuli.[2]

Many women played critical roles in South Africa's freedom struggle throughout the twentieth century, but despite the abundant academic studies,[3] biographies,[4] and autobiographies of women activists,[5] they are often presented as marginal or insignificant figures in struggle narratives because they usually did not participate in the public domain of politics and political parties.[6] And because they are generally perceived as directing their energies to family and domestic issues, they have been presented as "mothers, wives, sisters, and daughters" rather than activists in their own right.

An exception to this rule is Josie Mpama/Palmer, who played many public roles as a political activist. Nomboniso Gasa has accurately called her "an untidy hero for those who want to present a one-sided view of history. She demonstrated a fierce sense of power and of organizing women independently."[7] This biography is an attempt to narrate her life experiences and her contributions to the freedom struggle and how they add insight into our understanding of women's political lives.[8]

Josie's life sheds light on a number of issues. One is how her early life laid a foundation for issues she took on as a political activist. Josie was born in Potchefstroom less than a year after the end of the Anglo-Boer War (1899–1902) to a mixed-race woman and a Zulu man, a court interpreter whose views reflected those of the mission-educated black elite. After her parents divorced when she was seven, she was shuttled back and forth between different family members and had to find jobs as a domestic servant and seamstress. Her turbulent childhood taught her self-reliance and sensitized her as an adult to the need to protect both family and community.

In the late 1920s, she brought these concerns to her first experience in political activism: leading community protests that featured black women in Potchefstroom against an unpopular lodger's fee that undermined the stability and cohesion of black families. Standing up for black families and communities became her passion for the rest of her life.

The Potchefstroom protests exposed her to the Communist Party of South Africa (CPSA). She joined the party in 1928 and was the first black woman to play a prominent role in it. After moving in 1931 to Sophiatown, a black community in Johannesburg, she threw herself into CPSA organizing and resisting government repression. She took the remarkable step of traveling to the Soviet Union in 1935 to receive training at a Communist International (Comintern) school. The CPSA had been crippled by internal ideological disputes, and a Comintern commission called on her to testify at a dramatic hearing in Moscow that turned out to be a life-and-death showdown between CPSA factions.

Although a disciplined Communist Party member, Josie held independent views and was not reluctant about candidly expressing her dissatisfaction in the 1930s with the party on issues such as the content of its newspaper, its declining membership, its relations with Christians, and the difficulty of organizing black and white workers in joint actions. Nevertheless, with the party on the brink of collapsing in the late 1930s, she took strong stances on preserving it and opposing a controversial proposal to split it into black and white wings.

African National Congress (ANC) narratives dominate much of the scholarship on South Africa's freedom struggle. Josie's political life offers a different perspective. The CPSA was her primary political home, and that determined how she participated in leading black political organizations of the time: the ANC, the All-African Convention (AAC), and the Non-European Unity Front (NEUF).

She engaged publicly in local and national struggles. In keeping with her defense of family and community, she defended black townships such as Alexandra from being torn apart and expelled by the Johannesburg municipal council and was a leading figure in a national antipass campaign from 1943 to 1945 organized by the CPSA and the ANC.

Josie engaged in gendered politics. Most black women involved in political issues operated on the margins of male-dominated black organizations. Highly critical of the patriarchal attitudes that hindered black women from actively participating in politics, she was an outspoken advocate for women's social equality and encouraged black women to become more involved in issues of direct relevance to them: high rents, beer brewing, pass laws, police raids, education, health care, high bus fares, and the protection of black communities from forced removals and evictions. She did not see defending family structures and livelihoods as defining women as mothers and homemakers or a retreat from public life but as a way of mobilizing them politically.

During the 1930s and 1940s, Josie's views evolved on how black women should relate to black men in political initiatives. Initially she supported women working cooperatively with men in political organizations but then shifted to women forming autonomous organizations such as the Daughters of Africa. By the end of the 1940s, she was one of the founders of the Transvaal All-Women's Union, which advocated women of all racial groups joining together in one organization.

After the white National Party came to power in 1948 and began implementing the apartheid system, it intensified its attacks on the Communist Party, declaring it illegal and forcing it to disband in 1950. Josie remained involved in critical issues, especially protests against the Bantu Education Act and African women being forced to carry passes. In 1954, she was a leading figure in establishing the Federation of South African Women, which was open to women of all races.

Served a banning order by the government in 1955 and facing health challenges, she had to withdraw from formal politics and devoted her energy for the rest of her life to women's groups in the Anglican Church in her township, Mzimhlophe. She did not conform to the image of a communist as one opposed to religion. She remained loyal to the banned CPSA and did not see a contradiction between her beliefs as a Christian and as a communist. She was also an active presence in her neighborhood and drew on her knowledge of Afrikaner folk medicine to treat illnesses.

1

Family Matters

Josie Mpama/Palmer's chaotic childhood shaped her early life. As a court interpreter in Potchefstroom, her father held a privileged position in black society. But after her parents divorced when she was seven, she lacked an anchor in her personal life and struggled to find a semblance of family stability. Instead of being able to take advantage of the educational and social opportunities her father's status might have offered her, she was passed around from one family member to another and struggled to find a stable home. And, as a teenager, she had to provide for herself and her ailing mother by taking jobs as a domestic servant in white homes and as a seamstress. Her early life would make her even more concerned with creating and protecting stable family and community structures for black people when she entered political life in the late 1920s.

For a country whose past is so closely identified with rigid racial segregation, what is striking about many South African families is how racially mixed their lineages are. This was certainly the case with the family line of Josephine Winifred Mpama. Her father was Stephen Bonny Mpama, the son of Zulu parents, July and Anna

Figure 1.1. Stephen Mpama (*top row, on the left*), 1920s.
(Vesta Smith)

Mpama, who came from the Inanda mission reserve not far from Durban, which American Board missionaries had founded in the nineteenth century. Josie referred to her father as a "denationalised Zulu," by which she meant that his family were *amakholwa*, Christian converts who lived on mission stations and who attended mission schools and absorbed Western culture. Born in 1881 in Kroonstad, Orange Free State, Stephen moved with his family to Johannesburg after gold was discovered on the Witwatersrand in 1886. From about 1894, Stephen worked for a firm of chemists, Wilson and Coghill, in Langlaagte, to the west of Johannesburg.

Josie's mother was Georgina Garson Gasibone. Born around 1883, Georgina was the daughter of Johanna Garson, whose parents were a Mfengu woman and an Afrikaner man. Johanna married a moSotho, with whom she had two daughters, one of them Georgina. After her husband died, Johanna remarried, this time to a Scotsman by the name of Garson with whom she had three sons. They were raised "white," went to European schools, served in the South African Army during World War I, and eventually became strangers to their black half sisters.

Stephen and Georgina met in Johannesburg and were married in a civil ceremony on April 12, 1899, by the *veldcornet* (a field cornet was an official who performed military, administrative, and judicial duties) of Johannesburg and in a church by a Wesleyan Methodist minister on June 3, 1899. Her mother preferred that Georgina go live in the Cape Colony during the Anglo-Boer War while Stephen served as a guide in a British army infantry unit. After the war he returned to his old job at Wilson and Coghill for several years before taking up a position at Village Reef Gold Mining Company for fifteen months.

Following the war British colonial officials administered Potchefstroom, and Mpama was elevated to the apex of black colonial society when the Potchefstroom magistrate appointed him as a court interpreter at an annual salary of seventy-two pounds.[1] It was a position that educated Africans held in high esteem. As a young man in the Transkei before embarking on a law career, Nelson Mandela set his sights on becoming an interpreter for a magistrate or the Native Affairs Department because the post "was a glittering prize for an African, the highest a black man could aspire to."[2] In the black reserves, Mandela added, "an interpreter in the magistrate's office was considered second only in importance to the magistrate himself."[3] The English-speaking magistrate relied heavily on a multilingual black interpreter in the courtroom because the judge, plaintiff, defendant, counsel, and witnesses might all speak different languages. Drawing on his personal experience as a court interpreter in Kimberley, the veteran ANC leader Solomon Plaatje explained that an interpreter fluent in many languages and with an intimate knowledge of the law was essential so that a white judge "should clearly understand the evidence in any case upon which he sits in judgement, and the only means he has of attaining this in Southern Africa is by possession of a good interpreter."[4]

Mpama fit the profile of many Africans educated at mission schools. Known as "school people," they expected that their education and professional accomplishments would qualify them to be treated as the equals of whites. Mpama valued Africans advancing themselves through education. Because Africans who sought a college education could not have one in southern Africa, they went instead to the United Kingdom and the United States. To remedy this, in 1906, with 150 white and black delegates from all over South Africa, Mpama attended the Inter-State Native College Convention at Lovedale, the premier secondary school for Africans in the eastern Cape, which started the discussions for establishing an institution of higher education for black students, Fort Hare College (subsequently a university), a decade later.[5]

The school people also hoped that the British would not only preserve the qualified franchise for Africans and "Coloureds" (the apartheid-era term for people of mixed race) in the Cape Colony but also introduce it to their other South African colonies. School people were firm believers in bringing about change through constitutional means, but when a draft of the South Africa Act was released that proposed a constitution for a Union of South Africa that would keep political power in white hands, Africans from around the region met in Bloemfontein in 1909 to establish the South African Native Convention (SANC).[6] After a SANC delegation sent to London to appeal to British officials achieved nothing, Africans began discussing the creation of an organization that would unify their organizations. Mpama attended meetings of the Orange Free State Native Congress and the SANC in August 1911 that laid the foundation for the establishment of the South African Native National Congress in 1912.[7]

While Mpama's professional and political life was taking off, his personal life was in turmoil. Georgina and Stephen lost three children at birth before Georgina gave birth to Josephine—nicknamed "Josie" by her father—on March 21, 1903. According to Stephen, he and Georgina lived "happily" until 1908, when their relationship deteriorated and they divorced. Their divorce proceedings were messy, with both sides offering very different explanations

Figure 1.2. Baby photo of Josie Mpama/Palmer. (Palmer family album)

for why the marriage collapsed. Stephen's version was that his wife had cheated on him. After he and a policeman caught his wife in bed with another man, he initiated divorce proceedings. Georgina countered by accusing Stephen of raping a woman. As a result, she took Josie and went to stay with her mother in Sophiatown, a black township in Johannesburg. After returning to Potchefstroom in April 1909, she claimed that when they were staying with her uncle, Stephen assaulted her. Stephen admitted as much but testified that he was provoked by catching her in bed with another man. The circuit court judge sided with Stephen and ruled that Georgina had committed adultery. He awarded Stephen half of their communal property, damages of fifty pounds, and, most important, custody of Josie.[8]

The fallout from her parents' bitter split scarred Josie's childhood and certainly shaped her yearning as an adult for a stable home and family life and her compassion for children neglected by or alienated from their families. Interestingly, her personal account of her youth is a sad story of rancor, turbulence, and abandonment.[9] Her memory of the outcome of her parents' divorce was at odds with the court record. She believed the court had stipulated she could stay with her mother until she decided with which parent she wanted to live. She remembered leaving Potchefstroom with her mother on a train, and as her father was in the process of saying good-bye, he suddenly reached in the window and pulled her out. While her mother continued to fight for custody, she remained with her father in his five-room home in the Potchefstroom location.[10]

Stephen brought in a young man to look after her while he was at work, but after her mother protested that arrangement, her father employed a young woman. He then sent Josie to stay with his eldest sister, who lived a few miles from Josie's mother in Johannesburg. There she claimed she was treated poorly—clothes her mother sent her ended up being given to her aunt's daughter, for example. After Georgina brought a formal complaint to a court, her father took Josie back to Potchefstroom and called on his younger sister to stay with her.

This arrangement did not work any better. Josie claimed that she was treated as if she were "in jail." She was not allowed to play with her friends at school. On one occasion she ran away from home and met up with a group of her friends who were searching in a field for cow manure to use as cooking fuel. She had the shock of her life when what they thought was a pile of manure turned out to be a curled-up snake. She fled home, where she found that her father and other family members were frantically looking high and low for her because they thought her mother had kidnapped her. "Now instead of father scolding me for my wrong doings he took me on his lap and wept together with me as was his habit."[11]

Once it became clear that Stephen's sister could not look after her, Josie was shipped to the home of her uncle, Josiah Jolly Mpama, at Robinson Deep Mine in Johannesburg. "Life in that house," as she described it, "was something unheard of." In Potchefstroom she had attended an English-medium school, but at her new school, run by German-speaking Lutheran missionaries, English classes were held only a few times a week. Moreover, her aunt treated her abysmally, even withholding her food for lunch at school. Her uncle was aware of this, and he often slipped her food or money so she could buy lunch. His wife would also thrash Josie with a *sjambok* for the slightest offense, but after her uncle beat his wife so badly after one spanking that a doctor had to treat her, Josie was never again beaten when he

was at home.[12] His wife also forced Josie to help her sell wine illegally to mine workers. Josie's responsibility was to keep an eye out for "the detectives who if I see them coming should give her a warning."

Josie's mother came to visit her occasionally on Sundays, but since her aunt was always present, Josie was afraid to speak up about her treatment. When her mother decided to remarry, she bought a nice outfit for Josie, but on the wedding day her aunt refused to let her bathe, dressed her in a plain frock, and made excuses for not attending the wedding reception.

One day Josie was surprised when Georgina unexpectedly showed up at the school gate. She asked Josie if she wanted to come and live with her—something she had always hoped for. Her mother wrote a note to Josiah and his wife: "Don't look for [Josie]. I have taken her. She is at my place and I shall only hand her up when the highest court in the land compels me too [sic]."[13] A few days later Stephen arrived at Josie's granny's house, where they were staying. He spoke to her in isiZulu and told her that she had to go with him, but this time she "blankly refused and made him understand that I am now with mother and intend to stay with [her]."[14] When her father grabbed her by the arm, she clung fiercely to a door and screamed so loudly that others intervened to separate them. Later her grandmother showed her father the bundle of clothes she was wearing when her mother fetched her at school. It contained "boots that had no soles. Socks that had just the up's and the feet

rags, bloomers that had so many windows that one could see the whole earth without opening one."[15] Stephen was so ashamed to learn this that he gave up on trying to keep her, even though his relatives swore that they would not "leave their blood with bushmans."[16] They were true to their word, for several weeks later they attempted to drag her out of the house. This time her mother's husband and her brothers jumped into the fray. A fistfight broke out, and her father's relatives were ejected from the premises. The fight then went to the courtroom, where her mother was charged with stealing a child. The case exposed all the unpleasant things her uncle and aunt had done to her, and she was allowed to stay with her mother at her grandmother's place.

In 1917, Josie's mother's legs began weakening, and her husband urged her and Josie to go back to Potchefstroom. He promised to support them with his job in Johannesburg. They bought a three-room house with a small garden. Josie attended school, while her mother earned money washing clothes for white families. But when her mother's health worsened and she became an invalid, her husband reneged on his promise to look after them. Josie had to pitch in to wash and iron clothes on the side, and on Saturdays she cleaned the home of an elderly white woman.

Eventually her need to support her mother forced her to leave school and serve an apprenticeship with a tailor. In 1918, she and her mother moved to Doornfontein in Johannesburg, where they rented a room. Josie found work at an Indian tailor shop making button-holes and hand sewing. She also learned how to make trousers. But, always on the lookout for better-paying positions, she became a domestic servant for an elderly white couple. And knowing that cooks were paid a bit more, she learned enough, "with the aid of cooking books and recipes in newspapers," to find work as a servant and cook. She even polished floors, despite the toll it took on her knees and legs.

Working for a family of Russian Jews, she learned for the first time about the communist revolution of 1917. They "spoke about a revolution in that country and me, not knowing anything about politics and the birth of a new world, took no notice of what they were speaking about. Until 1928 when I got an idea of the revolution of which they spoke."[17]

Josie had her first child, Carol, with a Coloured man in Doornfontein in 1920, but she kept her maiden name. Around the time of the Rand Rebellion in 1922, when a white mine workers' strike almost brought Johannesburg to its knees, Josie, Carol, and her mother moved back to Potchefstroom and stayed in Stephen's comfortable house in the location surrounded by fig and apple trees. She gave birth to a second daughter, Francis, by another man in 1926.[18]

Although her childhood was rough, she acknowledged in an interview late in her life that she "learnt the value of doing things myself instead of always depending on the next person."[19]

While Josie and her mother were eking out a living, Stephen was doing well as an interpreter at the magistrate's court until a reorganization of staff led to his being retrenched in May 1912. After that he was used on a temporary basis.[20] He was a highly respected figure in Potchefstroom. In 1915, the local magistrate described him this way: "I may add that so far as this particular Native is concerned I can only say that in regard to linguistic accomplishments, civility, sobriety, general behavior and ability, he is altogether exceptional."[21] But in late 1916, his world was turned upside down when he was charged with knowingly receiving stolen property.

The case revolved around some sheets of corrugated iron that another black person, John Konden, had stolen from his employer and various other people and sold to Mpama in August 1916. Konden claimed that Mpama bought the goods knowing they were stolen. He testified that Mpama had seen him in front of the courthouse and asked him if he had any sheets of corrugated iron for sale. Because Mpama made it clear to him that he did not want to buy costly material from a white person, Konden inferred that Mpama did not care how he procured the material. He then stole the iron sheets as well as pipes and gutters. After delivering the goods to Mpama's home during the day, Mpama upbraided him for not bringing them at night. Then, when Konden was caught stealing some doors, he confessed to the police that Mpama had paid him for the sheets in front of the post office.

Mpama's version of his dealings with Konden was very different. He said he was tending his garden at his home when Konden came by and asked him why he did not put a furrow under the bridge in his garden so that water could flow easier. Konden offered to sell him materials for the furrow. When he arrived several days later with some secondhand sheets of corrugated iron in a handcart, Mpama bought five of them and placed them in his backyard.

The investigating officer, Detective Robert Glass, questioned Mpama about where he had bought the iron sheets. Put on the defensive, Mpama first denied knowing Konden at all. Then, when Glass said that he would search Mpama's home, Mpama admitted that Konden had given him one piece of piping as a present. After going to Mpama's house, Glass found some of the stolen property, which had identifying marks, in the backyard. When Glass asked Mpama a second time if he had purchased any property from Konden, Mpama swore again that he had not. Glass said that if he found out that Mpama was lying, then he would be arrested. After ascertaining that the material was stolen, he arrested Mpama who, as a result, was suspended from his interpreter's job.

After reviewing the evidence, the magistrate found Mpama guilty on October 5 and sentenced him to three months in jail. He suspended the sentence on condition of good behavior over the next three months. But, because of the conviction, the court had no alternative but to dismiss him from his post as interpreter.

Mpama appealed to the secretary for justice to overturn the conviction and reinstate him to his post. One wonders whether white officials had used Konden, who had been convicted five times for theft, to undermine Mpama because of his involvement in local and national politics. Indeed, once Mpama became aware of Konden's criminal record, he argued that the presiding magistrate should have dismissed the case, and he asked the secretary to review the trial evidence carefully. Mpama received strong backing from members of the Potchefstroom Side Bar and the Wesleyan Methodist minister, Reverend Whitehouse, who wrote the secretary calling for Mpama's reinstatement.[22] He pointed out Mpama's reputation for honesty from all quarters. "He may have been foolish but I think everyone is agreed that his character remains unsullied." Despite these letters of support, the secretary replied that he could not intercede on Mpama's behalf because he had been found guilty of a crime and thus had to leave the service.

In the meantime, Stephen had remarried around 1915.[23] He met his new wife, Clara Emma (1893–1980), while she was visiting an aunt in Potchefstroom. Her mother was of mixed Sotho and European parentage, and her father was thought to be a Griqua chieftain. She had a fourth-grade education,[24] and though she was largely self-educated, she could read and write well and kept up with the newspapers. The couple's first of four daughters, Marcy Elizabeth, was born on April 15, 1917.

Stephen eventually found employment after his brother Josiah, a clerk at the Robinson Deep Mine at the bottom of Eloff Street in downtown Johannesburg, unexpectedly died at the age of forty-three in October 1917. After mine officials invited Stephen to take over his brother's position,[25] he built a wood-and-corrugated-iron home in the residential area reserved for married African clerks.[26] In the homes of Stephen and his wives, the primary language was Afrikaans, but Clara Emma also spoke English and insisted that her daughters use it exclusively in public.[27] An unabashed admirer of British royalty, she would embarrass her children by insisting that they dress up and stand at such prominent viewing places as in front of the Rand Club when a member of the British royal family was visiting Johannesburg.

In Johannesburg, Stephen fit comfortably into the social network of the African social and political elite. George Montshioa, an advocate and a founder of the South African Native National Congress, and Isaiah Bud-M'belle, chief interpreter of the Supreme Court of Griqualand West at Kimberley, were godfathers to two of his children. Josie's half sisters remembered their family mixing with the leading lights of the time, such as Sol Plaatje. Stephen was active in the Transvaal Native Mine Clerks' Association, which he served as chair for several years;[28] the Joint Council of Europeans and Natives, which promoted interracial cooperation; and the Bantu Men's Social Centre, a social, cultural, and athletic hub in downtown Johannesburg established in 1924 that catered to educated Africans.

Stephen's children with Clara Emma recollected few stories about Stephen because they were so young when he died. They do remember him as a very strict person who expected his wife to set the table for tea at four o'clock sharp. Josie told them that he was highly intelligent and "a swanky old chap" who carried a hankie in his pocket to buff his shoes.

Stephen was forty-five when he died on May 3, 1927, at the Robinson Deep Mine Hospital.[29] An indication of his stature is that his funeral drew three hundred people, including officials of the Transvaal Native Mine Clerks' Association; compound *indunas*; leaders of the Joint Council of Europeans and Natives, such as R. V. Selope-Thema and Selby Msimang; T. D. Mweli-Skota, representing the ANC; and a Mr. Devenish, who promised that Stephen's "widow and children would never be in want so long as he was Compound Manager of Robinson Deep."[30] Indeed, the family was allowed to stay in their home at the mine until they moved to Vrededorp in the early 1940s. Clara Emma made ends meet working as a seamstress, upholsterer, and housekeeper for white employees at the mine. After they later moved to Vrededorp, she was employed at a boys' school in Mountain View (now Parktown Boys' High School).

At his death Stephen had achieved a reputation as a model of respectability and a voice of moderation. The next year, his daughter Josie joined the Communist

Party in Potchefstroom, where she became a radical proponent for confronting white power head-on through grassroots organizing.

2

A Fighting Location

Although Potchefstroom was a small town in the western Transvaal where segregation and white domination were deeply entrenched, its black residents had a long record of standing up for their rights and challenging unjust regulations. Josie's baptism into politics came in the late 1920s when residents of Potchefstroom's black location battled white municipal authorities over a host of oppressive regulations, the most hated being the lodger's permit, which required residents to pay a fee for anyone over the age of eighteen, including their own children, staying in their homes. Residents of the location, with women such as Josie in the forefront, put up a vigorous challenge to the permit and virtually shut down the town briefly in 1930.

Vital organizational and legal support for the challenges was provided by the Communist Party of South Africa. Josie, who married one of the CPSA's organizers, Edwin Thabo Mofutsanyana, joined the party in 1928, and it was to be her primary political home until the South African government outlawed it in 1950. Although the Potchefstroom protests achieved little in the

A Street in the Kaffir Location, Potchefstroom. S. A.

Douglas Smith.

Figure 2.1. A street in Makweteng Location, Potchefstroom, 1904. (Postcard in Robert R. Edgar collection)

end, they were a critical experience that shaped her political life and views after she and Edwin were chased out of Potchefstroom and moved to Johannesburg in 1931.

The Place of Sod

Potchefstroom's white *stadsraad* (town council) had established the black location Makweteng ("Place of Sod") in 1888 on very generous terms to its black standholders, who paid an annual fee of ten shillings for stands on a perpetual lease, which could be passed on to their children. Many of the stands had ample kitchen gardens and orchards.[1]

After the Anglo-Boer War, British colonial officials residing in Potchefstroom took over administration of Makweteng and began attempting to undermine the residents' rights by restricting tenure to a monthly basis with a rent of ten shillings per month. Location residents successfully challenged British authorities by bringing a case in 1905 to the Supreme Court, which ruled that since the British had not officially proclaimed Makweteng a location, the prewar regulations still stood. However, the following year the British authorities, despite the continuing opposition of location residents, introduced a new proposal for leasing stands for fifteen years at a monthly rental of four shillings.[2] *Indian Opinion,* which championed the rights of Indian traders in towns such as Potchefstroom, called the official intervention a "breach of faith," a reversal of their promise to maintain the prewar status of black people. The newspaper commented: "Europeans are terrified lest he [an African] should own land in his own name. He is labeled and marked, stigmatized and insulted. At nine o'clock at night, a lugubrious bell reminds him of his permanent inferiority to the white man, and warns him, like a criminal, to depart from the holy precincts of the towns to his locations."[3]

In 1908, location residents formed the Basotho Committee, which delegated Stephen Mpama, L. R. Muthle, and George Mtombela to conduct an interview with Transvaal's minister of native affairs, Johann Rissik, to remind him about the rights that location residents had to land and the annual rental agreement that they believed carried over from the late nineteenth century. They were concerned that the town council was not recognizing these rights.[4] The committee agreed to accept the minister's decision, which supported some individuals' claims to stands but disallowed others. That same year, the town council "gained the legal right to force any black person not living on the premises of a white employer to reside in the location."[5]

The conflict between location residents and the town council was reignited several years after the Transvaal became part of the Union of South Africa in 1910. In 1912, the Potchefstroom Town Council appointed a new location superintendent, a Mr. Dormyl, whose primary responsibility was to raise more money from location residents by collecting arrears on rents and sanitation fees, which they had resisted paying. The first time he met with township residents, on February 1 after arriving on his bicycle, he immediately began demanding passes from the men. He then told residents that they had to reregister and that the names and occupations of people living on stands had to be stated on the yearly stand permit. Residents complained to the town clerk about his attitude:

> Sir, is it right that a gentleman or Supt. should use
> such words if we had known he was the Supt. and
> had come in a better manner we are sure he (the boy)
> would of showed more civility. We are coloured but
> we know how to respect our superiors. But the way
> the new Supt. came and spoke to us and the words
> used we took him to be one of the many which knock
> about the location.[6]

Dormyl continued his boorish behavior by roaming around the location, knocking over water containers and cooking pots and entering people's homes without warning.

The local magistrate added fuel to the conflict by ruling that boys and girls over the age of fourteen had to take out permits to live in the location. Previously standholders could take out an annual permit that covered all members of their family and any lodgers. Residents interpreted the new rule as targeting women and girls for control under the pass laws that regulated where blacks could live, move, and work.

Dormyl followed up by threatening to sell the stands of any resident who had not paid up their rental arrears by April 10. On March 16, police raided the location before dawn and arrested twenty-three girls and seven boys, who all received a fine of one pound or a sentence of ten days in jail unless they took out a permit within ten days. Taking up the cause of the residents, an Anglican priest, Frederic Sharman, encouraged them not to pay their taxes or take out new residential permits until an appeal of the new regulations was heard in the Supreme Court. "The natives of this location," he asserted, "are all prepared to go to prison rather than submit."[7] The legal adviser to the town council accused Sharman of being responsible for creating the unrest in the location by putting "these natives into a state of ferment, even rebellion, to defy the Superintendent and the law and that your action can never bring about that point desired: viz: to have friendly cooperation."[8]

With women in the lead, location residents made several appeals to higher authorities. One was to the Native Affairs Department, whose acting secretary wrote the town clerk questioning why local officials thought it was necessary to add stricter controls, since the regulation had not been followed for some years. A petition, headed by Rachel Moloto, to Lord Gladstone, the British governor-general, detailed how the raid of March 16 had generated fear within the community:

> The Superintendent has the power at any time to refuse to renew our permits without stating any reason, and we have no right to appeal, so that if we continue to stay with our fathers and mothers, or our children, he or his Police boys, may arrest us in any place, at any time of the day or night, and drag us off to prison. . . . We pray for your noble Lordship's mercy and consideration of our prayers and cry to you.[9]

When the Supreme Court agreed to hear an appeal of the regulation by Dora Magati and sixteen others, Judge J. P. de Villiers wondered why not getting a permit could be a punishable offense. The court upheld the residents' objections by ruling that the town council and the superintendent should have given the residents a warning before they imposed any new regulations.[10] That was a victory for the township. The Native Affairs Department also dispatched a magistrate to mediate between the town council and location leaders. His solution was for the town council to stop enforcing the rule requiring boys and girls over the age of fourteen to have a permit. In October 1912, the Native Affairs Department went further by specifying that women in the location did not have to have a permit. These rulings kept an uneasy peace for a decade.[11]

In 1925, the national census put Potchefstroom's population at 13,363, comprising 8,180 whites, 4,241 Africans, 224 Indians, and 708 Coloureds.[12] In the location most blacks were seTswana speakers, but a significant number were Oorlams, blacks who had acculturated to Afrikaner culture and whose home language was Afrikaans. Because white farmers in the neighboring countryside were experiencing hard times, many black farmworkers had moved into town where there was already high unemployment, partly because the "civilized labor" policy of Prime Minister J. B. M. Hertzog's government was aimed at ensuring employment for poor whites. This policy lowered the wages for black domestic servants in white homes.

To control Potchefstroom's growing black population, the town council relied on the government's recently enacted Urban Areas Act of 1923, which was designed to allow town councils to regulate the administration of Africans living in urban areas, through establishing segregated locations for them, controlling their influx into urban areas, establishing advisory boards, and creating "native" accounts into which went revenues from beer-hall sales, rents, fines, and fees. Municipal councils had the discretion to decide which of the provisions to enact, and Potchefstroom's town council tried to implement most of them.[13]

Throughout the 1920s, the battles between location residents and the location superintendent and town council escalated as more and more restrictions and fees were imposed on location residents. In 1923, the location superintendent, complaining about a younger class of blacks becoming uncontrollable and making a ruckus in town, imposed a 10:00 p.m. curfew to quell unrest.[14]

The town council also levied a series of measures that directly affected women and their families. The Night Pass Ordinance, requiring black women to carry passes between 10:30 p.m. and 4:00 a.m., was put into effect on June 1, 1925.[15] That same year a fee of ten shillings and sixpence was imposed on location residents to pay for laying water pipes. Because the standards for clean water had been tightened and improved, many wells for water had been closed. New pipes meant water could become accessible closer to people's homes, but if they were shut down, people had to walk a mile to find a source of water.

Because many location women earned their income washing clothes for white families, the new levy directly affected them. On September 28, 1927, a procession of two hundred black women, marching in columns of four and carrying a red, white, and blue banner with "For Mercy" inscribed on it, went to see the magistrate,

Figure 2.2. Washing clothes, Makweteng Location, Potchefstroom, 1905. (Postcard in Robert R. Edgar collection)

who explained that the municipality was following rules set by officials in Pretoria. The town council was improving water standards to lessen the infant mortality rate caused by bad well water, and it was not raising rates for washing water but for gardens.

The protesters voiced their disagreement. One retorted that they had been drinking the well water for many years without ill effects, while "another asked whether it was worse for their children to die from drinking bad water or from starvation if they could not have a garden."[16]

The issue that touched off the most vigorous protests was the lodger's fee. The Native (Urban Areas) Act encouraged town councils to upgrade facilities in locations and offer new services, but they typically had to be paid for by raising fresh sources of revenue from location residents. A key way was the lodger's permit, "a licence issued by a municipality to a person who lived in a hired room or rooms in the house of another, including any male child above eighteen years of age or adult female or daughter of the registered owner of a house."[17] The permit's objective was twofold: to control and regulate blacks in urban areas and, in the case of Potchefstroom's location account, to cover a large deficit that would otherwise have had to be made up by white residents.[18]

Wherever the lodger's permit was introduced in South Africa, Africans deeply resented it because it undermined the integrity and cohesiveness of black family life by requiring any children over the age of eighteen of registered householders to take out a monthly permit to live with their parents. This often compelled them to take up employment at very cheap wages or to leave their homes for other urban areas such as nearby Johannesburg—in which case their families lost their incomes. Stand owners also lost rental income from lodgers.

A black newspaper, the *African Leader*, published an indignant editorial in 1933 that highlighted how the lodger's permit had undermined the African family's moral code: "Africans have a definite moral code of their own, especially in the upbringing of children. One of their important rules or moral codes lies in the strength of parental control. A child is never free from it until he or she is emancipated." The editorial went on to argue that the permit split the "family in a most savage and inhuman way" by taking away the right of parents "to supervise, tend and nurse the character of their children.[19]

The town council relied on Andries Johannes Weeks, hired as the location superintendent in December 1926, to keep residents in line. If moviemakers were casting the role of a callous brute, they could not have chosen better than Weeks. He zealously took up his new position and swaggered around the location terrorizing people with his sjambok. He was constantly on the lookout for ways in which the town council could squeeze more revenue from location residents. After visiting Boksburg in 1930 to study how the government there maximized the collection of lodger's fees, he concluded that the Potchefstroom municipality was being shortchanged and could increase its ten-pound monthly revenue from residents by 400 percent.[20]

By May 1928, location residents had become so fed up with Weeks that 1,232 of them signed a petition calling him "as not a fit and proper person to hold the office of Superintendent." They listed a litany of complaints: his inability to speak any African languages contributed to misunderstandings between him and residents; he regularly whipped residents with his sjambok; he harshly treated people who did not whitewash their homes; he arrested people for vagrancy; he led indiscriminate night searches of people's homes; and he routinely broke up their meetings. They pointed out his "insulting manner towards our women" and that he used the provisions of the Urban Areas Act "as weapons to deprive us of the ordinary rights of mankind, to security of person and property" instead of using the regulations to improve the lot of the people. They concluded, "In general we are voicing the united protest of our people against the excessive hardship and totally uncalled for suffering which is the lot of the residents of this location."

Copies of the petition were sent to the town council as well as the prime minister, the ministers of justice and of native affairs, and the press. Not surprisingly Weeks summarily dismissed their complaints as communist propaganda. "In my opinion," he charged, "the petition is a very good example of Communist intrigue and misrepresentation."[21]

The petition made no impact on white authorities, and Weeks intensified his campaign of terror against location residents. For instance, Benjamin Mohlomi, an assistant teacher at the Dutch Reformed Church school, complained to the mayor that Weeks had it in for him. He had used abusive language toward him, threatened to "break his neck," and leaned on Mohlomi's school to dismiss him. Mohlomi complained that one time he was standing outside school before classes one day when "all of a sudden [Weeks] pointed [at] me vigorously with his finger and called me a Baster [bastard] etc. I am afraid this seems to be a continual practice and has grown into a habit now."[22] Weeks's sjamboking of a black woman led to even more protests.[23]

One weapon that location residents effectively wielded to combat Weeks and the town council was the legal system, but the key was finding an organization that would bring cases to court. The Transvaal African National Congress and the Industrial and Commercial Workers' Union (ICU) had branches in Potchefstroom, but they were not able to organize effectively. In May 1926, an ICU organizer Sidney Buller, who had applied to the council to stay in the location, was turned down. Buller did not pull any punches about why he had been sent to Potchefstroom. "I came here to agitate amongst the natives in respect of the trade, stories and their services with the white population. . . . I am here to agitate in respect of the economic wages." He added, "We drive to prosecute the master and compel him to pay a month's wage"[24] Not surprisingly, F. van der Hoff, the location superintendent at the time, did not consider Buller "a fit and proper person because he is an agitator" who had no employment or a place to live.

Although faced with the same opposition to their sending organizers, the CPSA, whose lawyers were prepared to take on court cases, proved to be the most effective organization for mobilizing protests. The party had a presence in Potchefstroom since 1926 when two of its African members asked for permission to live in the location. After the superintendent refused to issue them lodger's permits, they unsuccessfully approached the town council. As a last resort, they appealed to the local magistrate, U. G. Horak. The party's attorney argued that the location superintendent had not used proper discretion and had refused them permission solely because they were members of a party that was still legal. The magistrate agreed with his logic and ruled that since the defendants had not been doing anything subversive in the location, they should not have been penalized just because they were CPSA members. Since the superintendent had not taken all the facts into consideration, Horak directed him to issue permits to the party members.[25]

This was not the last time that party lawyers succeeded in challenging the authorities in Potchefstroom. After location activists approached the central party office in Johannesburg about establishing a branch in Potchefstroom, the party dispatched T. W. Thibedi, one of the first African communists, and Douglas and Molly Wolton in March 1928 to speak at a rally that drew a crowd of about a thousand. Thibedi reminded the attendees that the British had promised them many things during the Anglo-Boer War in exchange for their support:

> You people were well-to-do before that war, but your property was taken away from you. You were given pieces of paper and were promised that your property will be restored to you after the war. Was your property returned to you after the war? No! You were poor people when the war was over and you are being kept poor.[26]

A white policeman then disrupted Thibedi's speech and asked him whether he had permission to hold a public meeting in the location. He then took Thibedi to the magistrate's office where he was charged with convening a meeting without a permit and inciting racial hostility, an offense made illegal by the recently passed Native Administration Act. Thibedi was represented by the party's chair, Sidney Bunting, who argued that the charge did not precisely detail what the offense was and that Thibedi's speech had not created any hostility between the races. Accepting Bunting's line of reasoning, the magistrate backed the right of free speech and dismissed the charge, stating that if Thibedi and the party operated in a constitutional manner, they had a right to challenge what they saw as unjust laws.

The party celebrated the victory by immediately organizing a rally in Potchefstroom's market square. But white vigilantes, who were ever present at black meetings, were so incensed by Wolton's speech that they started roughing him up. Blacks and whites in the crowd then turned on each other and touched off a melee.[27]

Thibedi's triumph in court was a demonstration that the party could deliver and was the starting point for establishing a party branch in the location. Six weeks later the Potchefstroom branch was claiming seven hundred members. A month after that, Bunting inflated the figure to four thousand.[28] In June, Edwin Thabo Mofutsanyana and Shadrach Kotu were dispatched to organize the branch properly and to launch a "school

Figure 2.3. Edwin Mofutsanyana, 1940. (*Inkululeko*)

for the purpose of extending the knowledge of party work amongst the members." They opened an office outside the location.

Born in 1899 in Witzieshoek in the Orange Free State, Mofutsanyana had worked in the Western Cape before attending Bensonvale Institution in the Herschel District of the Eastern Cape for four years, where one of his classmates was Albert Nzula, who was to become the first African general secretary of the CPSA.[29] Working as a clerk at the New Modderfontein mine in Benoni, Mofutsanyana became politicized by the African National Congress in the early 1920s. He joined the party in 1927 after his interest was piqued by a British communist, Jimmy Shield, who was speaking at a rally in Vereeniging. Mofutsanyana soon became an ardent communist, attending a party night school and throwing himself into CPSA campaigns. Shortly after being sent to Potchefstroom, he met Josie Mpama, a single woman with two daughters. The two fell in love and had a daughter, Hilda, the following year. We do not have any record of why and how Josie decided to join the protests, but she soon became one of the CPSA's most vocal leaders.

Several months after Mofutsanyana and Kotu arrived in Potchefstroom, Superintendent Weeks tried to expel the pair, and the town council attempted to ban all political meetings in the location. After Mofutsanyana and Kotu were arrested several times for staying in the location without permits, they were forced to sleep in the open veld. They turned again to the courts, and a sympathetic magistrate ruled that simply being a communist was not ample justification for their being declared "undesirable." Weeks was forced to issue them a permit allowing them to stay until the end of 1929.

The lodger's fee was Weeks's favored weapon for gaining greater control over every aspect of the lives of location residents. He successfully lobbied the Public Health Committee for a monthly fee of two shillings to be exacted on every lodger's permit, which was put into effect in January 1928. This allowed him to keep tabs on everyone living in the location. Those who did not pay would be prosecuted and expelled.

With the location already at a boiling point, the lodger's fee was the tipping point for activists such as Josie, who led campaigns against it. Protesters brought a test case in late 1928. The lawyer representing the accused argued that section 17 of the regulations under the Urban Areas Act authorized the municipal authority to levy charges for services on every registered occupier, but he maintained that since this was covered under the monthly levy of nine shillings on standholders, imposing an additional fee for the lodger's permit was excessive. Although the magistrate ruled against the accused, he did not impose a fine, but he advised location residents in the court that he believed the fee was reasonable.[30]

The confrontation escalated when Frank Molife, who had been born in the location, challenged the legality of the lodger's permit. After the magistrate ruled that the bylaw was valid, Molife's lawyer, T. Tom, appealed to the Supreme Court, which dismissed the appeal on December 5, 1929.[31] Eventually Molife and his wife and three children were evicted for not paying the lodger's fee,[32] and they were escorted to a place on the veld, where their furniture was dumped. This aroused the ire of the black community, which maintained that Molife but not his family should have been evicted. When a delegation approached the magistrate about this, he directed them to the town clerk, who then sent them to a council member, a Mrs. Nel, chair of the location committee. She said she could do nothing for the Molifes. Several hundred protesters decided to bring Mrs. Molife, the children, and their furniture back to the location. Weeks called in the police to deal with the group.

The protests turned violent on December 16, 1929. To commemorate Dingaan's Day and the freedom struggle against white domination, the party organized a rally and distributed an incendiary flyer to attract more people.[33] The flyer stated:

> Roll up in your thousands! African workers! You have
> no guns or bombs like your masters, but you have
> your numbers; you have your labour and the power
> to organize and withhold it. These are your weapons;
> learn to use them, thereby bringing the tyrant to his
> knees.[34]

Before the rally, Mofutsanyana caught wind of a rumor that an attempt was going to be made on his life. He thought that Weeks was deliberately spreading it to try to scare him off, so he kept the information to himself and told no one on the platform.[35] The meeting opened at 10:00 a.m., with about 500 Africans and 120 whites in the audience and twenty policemen monitoring the proceedings. As soon as Mofutsanyana started speaking, whites began heckling him. His interpreter, J. B. Marks, who was to become a party stalwart, was translating into Afrikaans, and he did not hold back. "I am surprised to see Europeans here who have come to cause trouble, whereas others are at home having their holiday." He asked why they were disrupting black meetings, while Africans refrained from interfering in any white meetings. As the whites hurled insults, Mofutsanyana saw someone pointing a gun at him, and he and Marks leaped off the stage to the ground. The man brandishing the gun was Joseph Weeks, the location superintendent's brother, who began shooting wildly into the crowd. Five blacks were injured in the ruckus. The most critically injured among them was Hermann Lithipe, who was attending the rally merely out of curiosity. He suffered a wound that became so severely infected that doctors had to amputate his leg. Then, on December 22, he suffered a heart attack and died.[36]

Learning of his death, Mofutsanyana addressed a rally next to the Methodist church, severely criticizing whites:

> It seems to be the policy of the ruling classes to
> shoot the nigger. These honourable hypocrites, these
> civilisers of the Black man, these people, under the
> shield of Christianity, told them that fear of the Lord
> was the beginning of knowledge. They had been
> shooting, they were shooting and they still intended to

shoot. The Black man should let them see that he had power though he had no machine guns, aeroplanes, or cannons. The Black man's power lay in his own hands.[37]

Drawing a connection between Christianity and communism, he stressed that both believed in equality and social justice and that Christ, like the Communist Party, stood with the outcasts and the oppressed and was prepared to stand up for people's rights. However, communists wanted to change things for the better now, not in the afterlife: "If we cannot show love in this world, then that beautiful place called Paradise is no use to us—to hell with it."[38]

Josie Mpama's response to Lithepe's shooting was succinct: "For hooligans to shoot a Native is but to break a black bottle and then congratulate themselves on being such good marksmen."[39] She was frustrated by the fact that blacks were not spurred to action by the shooting and that the judicial system treated whites with kid gloves. The police arrested Joseph Weeks and charged him with murder and fourteen other whites with public violence. But when their trial finally took place in mid-1930, Weeks was acquitted of murder. Although eight of the others charged with inciting public violence were found guilty, the magistrate let them off with a warning to keep away from black meetings.

The Dingaan's Day shooting set the stage for a series of dramatic protests in 1930. When Mofutsanyana's permit to stay in Potchefstroom expired in late 1929, a magistrate ruled that he could not extend it any further. In addition, Weeks escalated his persecution of "undesirables" and received permission from the town council to sell standholders' homes if they fell more than a month behind in their rent payments.

Josie became prominent in the protests in March 1929 when she joined a delegation that met with the Public Health Committee, the commandant of police, and the magistrate to challenge the harshness of the lodger's fee and Week's evictions.[40]

Things came to a head in 1930 when another batch of location residents was arrested on January 26 for not being in possession of lodger's permits. Mofutsanyana called for a total stay away from work, and Josie and other location women began making plans for shutting down the town. They formed a special strike committee that laid out a strategy for preventing black people from going to work on a Monday morning by placing pickets on all the three roads leading out of the location and organizing a march into town.

The women activists typically held their organizing meetings late at night. They "gathered by singing on the streets, moving from street to street until all the women had gathered."[41] Their style of mobilizing had all the fervor of an evangelical crusade of the Wesleyan Methodist Church, which was very popular among Potchefstroom blacks.[42] Josie, who was active in the church, described the scene in a report she produced while attending a communist school in Moscow in 1935:

The roads would be picketed by the masses on the day of trial. The picket usually started at 3 a.m. By 5 a.m. the police from the charge office would be there threatening the picketers that they would be arrested for abstracting [obstructing] the way and preventing the workers from going to work. The workers simply answered that the police surrended [surrounded] the location, arrested and kept the workers till 9—10 o'clock before they laid a charge. So is better for all to be arrested and enjailed [jailed]. In fact the police could never take action except for arresting me a few times but on account of mass pressure I was never convicted. . . .

The bugel [bugle] sounded which was the call for picketers from all four locations. Workers with babies on their backs came and men by 8 o'clock the location was empty as the Town Hall the town clerk told the protesters that the Superintendent was their father. This engage [enraged] the crowd. They stormed the Town Hall, where he had escaped into. Then Party called upon the location's inhabitants to down tools by evening troops had arrived from nearby towns. Martial law was declared, but the masses no longer knew their homes but stayed at the meeting day and night.[43]

When the historian Julia Wells interviewed Josie in 1977, she provided additional details. A few men who tried to bicycle through the women pickets were turned back. "One woman called them dogs, to which another replied, 'but at least dogs can bark.'" The women shamed the men: "Give us your trousers, we will take off our dresses."[44]

The women effectively sealed off the town. At 9:00 a.m., a procession of three hundred men and two hundred women marched from the location to the courthouse. White townsfolk were in a panic. Josie recollected, "By this time all the townspeople were going wild—their servants hadn't shown up for work and neither had anyone else. And now all the residents of the location were marching on the town *en masse*."[45]

When the protesters reached the courthouse, the magistrate told them, "Well boys, I believe you have some grievances." A Mr. Lefoko spoke for the demonstrators. They had gathered for one primary reason: "to protest against the lodger's permits, nothing more and nothing less." But they were also angered by the attitude of Weeks, who refused to meet them—indeed, he was not present at this meeting.

Native Affairs officials in Pretoria, concluding that the situation had spun out of control, dispatched D. W. Hook, the assistant secretary for native affairs, to intervene and to take evidence from all the parties. Arriving on the third day of the protests, Hook drove to the location and asked for protest leaders to meet him at 6:30 p.m. at the superintendent's office. To make sure that witnesses from the location could testify, Josie "posted the witnesses on various street corners in town, having them fetched at the appropriate moment. This prevented city officials from knowing in advance who would be appearing and pre-empted any further chance of interfering with the testimony." According to her, "only the Party's representatives were able to expose the municipality and the Superintendant [*sic*]." In any event, black members of the Location Advisory Board, who generally reflected moderate opinion and who were aware of how much out of step they were with township residents, refused to speak to the commission.

After hearing evidence for three days, Hook pointed out the obvious: the main complaints of the residents were the lodger's permits and the zealous way in which the superintendent carried out his duties. But Potchefstroom's mayor refused to rein in Weeks, saying that while the town council made the rules, it was not in charge of enforcing them.

Eventually a deputation from the location, consisting of one location representative, one member of the Location Advisory Board, and one member of the party, went to meet the secretary for native affairs. As a result, the permit was abolished. All strangers now had to do was report, and they would receive a permit free of charge.

Hook's official report was given to the town council but never made public. Eventually A. R. Wilmot, the local magistrate, met with location residents to provide a summary of Hook's recommendation. But residents were not pleased when he revealed that the report described Weeks as a "capable and efficient officer" and that Weeks should be given more time to deal with the disputes. Josie wrote John Allison, the secretary for native affairs, that location residents were "surprised" that Weeks was described in this manner, given all the "insults" and "assaults" he had committed against them.[46] When she requested a face-to-face meeting with Allison, he directed her to meet with the Potchefstroom magistrate, who would communicate their views to Pretoria.[47]

But the town council and Weeks were not receptive to any changes. They created a new committee, the Native Location Committee under the chairmanship of a Mrs. Nel, to oversee affairs in the location. They authorized Weeks to resume evicting people who were in arrears and to evict about a dozen people from the location who had failed to pay their lodger's fees for the last five months of 1929.[48]

However, protesters had their own strategy for defying the law. Many lodgers had been prosecuted for failing to pay the fee, and the magistrate had given them the choice of a fine of one pound or ten days in jail. Most chose to go to jail, a step that was in line with their strategy of passive resistance. Wilmot generally showed leniency toward the protesters who opted to be fined by giving them a month to pay it off or a lengthy grace period in which to settle their arrears. That led Weeks to press the town council to communicate to Wilmot about "his future conduct in dealing with these defaulters" and to inform him that his leniency was actually encouraging even more resistance.[49]

Then a deputation of women from the location went to see Wilmot "to protest against what was deemed to be the arbitrary and unjust ejectment of woman and children against who no legal process had been ordered." Although Wilmot agreed with them, he once again sent them to the town hall, where they were directed again to Mrs. Nel—with the same result. Wilmot's position was that his role was to "administer the law as he found it and that if the natives were dissatisfied with the law there were constitutional methods open to them to attempt to have it amended."

By March 1931, Weeks declared that he was not going to take any more cases to court unless a magistrate other than Wilmot was presiding. Because of Wilmot's actions, Weeks bitterly complained that "in some cases [he] has made me to look a fool in the presence of the natives and in one case as much as told me he did not believe me." Although he had collected five hundred pounds in lodger's fees in January 1931 alone, there were still arrears of one thousand pounds. Wilmot regarded the prosecutions on the lodger's fees as trivial and stated in court that the government had instructed him "not to send natives to gaol for trivial offences."[50]

The Native Location Committee adopted a resolution on September 4, 1931, recommending that Weeks should stop collecting lodger's fees for the first six months of the financial year "as the collection thereof will only cause a lot of complications and a great deal of dissatisfaction" and that the lodger's fees themselves should be abolished.[51]

In 1931, the town council officially proclaimed a location and reintroduced a permit law. This time some "good boys," as Josie called them, in the location held meetings and collected money for a case.[52] The party argued that because a location had been proclaimed, it was a waste of time and money to bring a court case that would go nowhere. Meanwhile the party was busy organizing location residents for action, while the "good boys and their followers" lost their case. According to Josie, "this proved to the masses that the Party was right."

The Department of Native Affairs recommended that women be allowed to run for seats on the Location Advisory Board. According to Josie, she and another woman party member, Johnson, received the most votes in the election, but Weeks refused to accept the results of the vote since he had selected his own board members.

At the end of 1931, Mofutsanyana and Mpama were evicted from the location. When she returned for visits, she was permitted to meet only her mother and no one else in the location. She recalled, "A private detective was appointed to watch me and when my time expired a sergeant came to see that I cleared out."

The pair's experiences in Potchefstroom taught them much about the challenges of organizing community struggles. One was how difficult it was to organize whites and blacks into a genuine multiracial movement.

Could they have a common class base and overlapping interests? Based on her experience in Potchefstroom, Josie questioned whether this was possible unless there was a lot of spadework educating people. She noted that in Potchefstroom there was an area in which poor whites lived next to the black location and that the two races mixed a lot. "They eat and drink with the natives. Help the natives in times of sickness." But when Weeks wielded race-baiting tactics to set the poor whites against the Communist Party, Mofutsanyana and Mpama could not win over any of the poor whites. "The party here was a purely native organisation and carried on work only among the natives." She later observed:

> Unity can be achieved between white and black. But what is necessary here is that we first organize the whites to such a stage where they will see what the cause of their poverty is. How they are to struggle against it. Then we should pick from the crowd those more conscious, have a private talk to them so as to test their feelings. When we find that we have a few who understand then we can begin to put to poor whites the native question.[53]

What motivated people to join the party? Party histories boast that it gained thousands of members in the late 1920s and early 1930s, but an accounting of who joined and why casts doubt on these figures. Eugene Dennis, the Comintern representative in South Africa, reported that a thousand people, the majority of them farmworkers who had recently settled in Potchefstroom, enrolled at one meeting. Their commitment to the party was suspect since they had joined without any understanding of party doctrine. Dennis acknowledged that the nucleus of the party in Potchefstroom actually consisted of only about twenty-five members.[54] In a party of about 129 members nationwide, Potchefstroom's formed the largest branch.[55]

A key to the party's success was its willingness to take on legal cases, especially over lodger's permits. The party overcame the skepticism of location residents about joining and paying dues to an organization that was perceived as led by whites and began registering members in droves through house-to-house visits and mass meetings. Mofutsanyana recollected:

> We were drafting everybody who joined. . . . So after I gave a speech, many people would flock and give their names. We would call them members of the Party. So we could have had hundreds and hundreds of them, but we had no way of organizing them. We had a big, loose Party and we called them Communists. . . . Of course, later when they understood what it was to be a Communist, then there was a change. In those days there was just a mass calling of people to join. Some of the people who came to us thought they were Communists because they had given us their names.[56]

Even though many of those who joined were not well versed in the party's beliefs, they saw no difficulty in joining and still participating actively in their churches. As Mofutsanyana put it, "Yes, you see those who joined the party at that time did not worry they were Christians or what. We were just taking them all. They became members of both the church and the Party. . . . Some of them drifted in and out. The Party was like a revolving door."[57] Or, as Moses Kotane later confirmed in a letter circulated to party members, the party in general "was something like a church congregation, very loose, politically illiterate and knew nothing about Communism save that it stood and fought for their rights."[58]

According to Josie, the professional look of a party organizer also could be a motivation for joining. She recollected one man "who recruited for these meetings for the Communist Party with great fervour. When one man asked him why he should join, the answer was given that he would be able to carry a briefcase, like the organisers do."[59]

To Josie, who joined the party in 1928, the party's primary objective was to organize protests and not to educate people about the intricacies of communist ideology or philosophy. She acknowledged that it was only after she went to Johannesburg that she was exposed to communist thinking.[60] Although communist ideology did not play an important role in attracting members to the party in the late 1920s, ideological disputes would nearly destroy it in the 1930s, as we shall see later.

While the Potchefstroom protests were still at a fever pitch, Mofutsanyana received a telegram in late

December from the party's central office in Johannes-burg directing him to go immediately to Durban after party organizer Johannes Nkosi and several others were killed in a clash there with police on Dingaan's Day. He lasted a few months before the authorities clamped down on his activities and expelled him from Natal. Josie was unhappy because the party's abrupt decision to pull Mofutsanyana from Potchefstroom had an ad-verse effect on their protests. She complained that for better or for worse, in Potchefstroom they at least "had a Party; the line may have been wrong, but neverthe-less we had forces when we called a demonstration. The people came out." She did not hesitate to pin the blame on officials at party headquarters in Johannesburg for undermining their work, and she criticized them for fa-voring urban centers over small towns and rural areas: "The Party did not care what happened, and when I was there, I was asked: why does the Party neglect us in this way? They were right. The same thing happened in other places. We had branches and secretaries who were active and then they are called away to the centre."[61]

Although Josie claimed that the party did not dis-patch anyone to take Mofutsanyana's place, it did send Joseph Sepeng to Potchefstroom on March 7, 1931. He promptly reported to Weeks and applied for a permit to reside in the location as a party organizer. Weeks asked him what his nationality was and what kind of man he was. Sepeng replied in Afrikaans that he was "a black man which means that he is a native." Weeks explained that he could not issue a permit to someone who did not carry a pass and that he was immediately calling the police to arrest him. When Sepeng appeared in court, he was fined for not having a pass, which he had destroyed. He approached Weeks again for a permit. Weeks turned him down for being "unfit, unproper and undesirable." Sepeng's appeal to the town council was also rejected.[62]

Josie's experiences with the Potchefstroom protests grounded her in how to deal with a range of practical issues: mobilizing township residents against unjust regulations and an oppressive superintendent, organizing under the banner of the Communist Party, the difficulty of bringing blacks and whites together in joint actions, and using gender issues to draw women into protests. She learned that black men and women could be drawn into action by focusing on the attacks on their livelihoods as well as their families, but she also witnessed the power of women in organizing and mobilizing people and saw that they were more prepared than men to take direct action to challenge white power. When Julia Wells asked Josie why women were more willing to engage in protest than men, her candid assessment was "Because men are cowards! They are afraid of losing their jobs."[63]

Although she would operate in the Johannesburg area without the same kind of community base she had had in Potchefstroom, she maintained her passion for protecting family and community. She would become a fiercely independent voice, articulating her criticisms of the Communist Party as well as the patriarchal attitudes that stifled women's involvement in political issues. And she learned that operating on the national and international level presented complex challenges.

Party Battles

After Josie, Edwin, and their family moved to Sophiatown in 1931, her CPSA activities immediately drew her into pitched battles with a government not only committed to the party's destruction but also to assaulting black people on a number of fronts: eradicating the small number of black voters in the Cape Province, ensuring that white farmers maintained access to cheap labor, and extending its control over the lives of blacks—especially women—who were migrating into urban areas in greater numbers.

During the 1930s, Josie was also concerned with ideological faction fighting within the CPSA that nearly brought about its collapse. When she traveled to the Soviet Union for a year of party training in mid-1935, the CPSA's internal squabbles drew her into a life-and-death showdown between rival factions as dictator Joseph Stalin was preparing to launch the "Great Terror"—arresting and executing hundreds of thousands of "enemies of the state" and shipping over a million more to prison camps.

Riotous Assemblies

During the 1920s, the National Party government of Prime Minister J. B. M. Hertzog was so concerned about protests by the Industrial and Commercial Workers' Union and the CPSA that Parliament passed the Native Administration Act in 1927 and the Riotous Assemblies Act in 1930 to quell dissent. The latter was designed to nullify a Supreme Court ruling in 1929 in a case involving CPSA chair Sidney Bunting that had affirmed the CPSA's right to freedom of speech. That allowed CPSA lawyers to continue to represent dissidents in protests, which they had effectively done in Potchefstroom. The act empowered the governor-general to crack down on any individual or group that was creating "feelings of hostility" between whites and other racial groups and gave the minister of justice, Oswald Pirow, the discretion to decide who was promoting such feelings. He could banish people from specific areas without recourse to the courts and forbid people from attending public meetings.[1] Wielding his broad powers, Pirow specifically targeted CPSA organizers and relied on the newly established South African Police's Special Branch unit to keep a watchful eye on party members and to dutifully report on their activities.

While CPSA members were being regularly arrested, Pirow's measures did not still Josie or the party, which held weekly rallies on the steps of the Johannesburg city hall. On September 18, 1932, with three hundred Europeans and twenty Africans present, Josie defiantly referred to her recent experiences in Potchefstroom: "She had been chased out of Potchefstroom by Pirow, but he could chase her where he liked, she would continue to tell the people how he is starving natives to death, and throwing them into gaol because they ask for their rights."[2] A few weeks later she chaired a meeting at the Trades Hall, where she again lambasted Pirow: "What I can tell you my comrades is that Pirow and his Imperialist friends are afraid of you being organized. I am sure we are more encouraged than what we were before."[3]

Speaking in November 1932 to a Sophiatown audience of Africans and whites, she launched an attack on the ever-present security police whose attendance, she felt, had kept down the numbers in the audience:

> They have not been asked to this meeting and yet they
> are standing at the door, waiting for the meeting to
> be over when they will demand your passes, which is
> all they can do, as you know they are half cocked. My
> advice to you is always attend our meetings as the time
> is coming when we will tell Pirow and his Police to go
> to Hell.[4]

On May Day 1933, before an estimated crowd of eight hundred Europeans and three hundred Africans, she shared a platform with CPSA members Issy Diamond, Willie Kalk, Eddie Roux, and John Gomas at the Johannesburg city hall. Josie "said it was useless for the working classes to make a distinction between white and black as the bosses were not concerned with the colour of the skin but, whether they could exploit and starve the workers to death. White women were being driven onto the streets to sell their bodies, and 'What the

77

hell did the bosses care.'"[5] Hecklers not only frequently disrupted her speeches but also those of others. A brawl broke out when a white man rushed at Kalk as he rose to speak.

The Red Mecca

Josie's most challenging experience in the 1930s came not in South Africa but in the Soviet Union when factional squabbles in the CPSA came to a head. The Soviet Union had established the Comintern in 1919 to promote revolutionary communism and to coordinate communist parties around the world, but in reality its policies served Soviet foreign policy objectives rather than being refined to fit local realities. In 1927, the Comintern aimed to tap into anticolonial and national liberation struggles. After consulting with some South African comrades, it came up with its own policy and directed the CPSA to adopt the Independent Native Republic thesis, which it thought would attract more black people into the party. The Native Republic was to be the first stage in a process that would lead to a socialist society serving workers and peasants. In practical terms, it meant black majority rule and the return of land to indigenous people, but it raised many questions about what exactly the policy meant, how it was to be implemented, and how whites, who then were a majority in the party, would fit in. Sidney Bunting opposed the Native Republic "for its racial exclusivity and nationalist orientation" and for precluding a role for white workers.

He instead proposed a slogan, "All power to the Soviets and workers and peasants—black and white."[6]

The Native Republic controversy touched off an intense power struggle within the party.[7] After visiting the Soviet Union in late 1930, Douglas Wolton, the CPSA's general secretary, returned with a Comintern directive to "bolshevize" the CPSA and to purge those who raised any objections to the Native Republic line. The following year he expelled party stalwarts such as Bunting, Solly Sachs, Thibedi, Bill Andrews, and Gana Makabeni for contending that the Native Republic marginalized white workers. Josie aligned herself with the faction supporting the Native Republic and denounced Makabeni at a meeting in December 1931: "Anyone who does wrong should be expelled no matter what his colour is."[8]

Later, in Moscow in 1935, while acknowledging her position, she expressed regret for the abrupt way Bunting had been ousted. Noting that he was an influential figure among blacks because he handled legal cases for free, she admitted that the party had erred by not explaining what errors Bunting had committed and why he had been expelled. The only notice of his expulsion appeared in the local party newspaper *Umsebenzi* (which had a limited circulation) without an adequate explanation. Josie said this had angered many people.[9]

Several years later the faction fighting over the Native Republic was still crippling the party. Moses Kotane, Eddie Roux, and John Gomas remained loyal to their interpretation of the Native Republic thesis, saying that it was the first stage toward the creation of a socialist state. Opposing them were Lazar Bach, J. B. Marks, and Edwin Mofutsanyana, who focused on the Native Republic's "socialist and class nature" and contended that it would lead to a socialist revolution.

The disputes had ramifications for the handful of South Africans studying in the Soviet Union. In 1923, the Communist Party of the Soviet Union had initially established the University of the Toilers of the East (KUTV) to train party cadres who came from the Soviet Union's eastern border areas. After being placed under the Comintern, KUTV recruited black students from the United States, the West Indies, and South Africa, who were sent to Section 9, otherwise known as the "Negro Section" of the Anglo-American Sector. South Africans, both black and white, began traveling to Moscow for training in the late 1920s.[10] Eventually fourteen studied at KUTV, including the CPSA's general secretary, Albert Nzula (who tragically died in Moscow in 1934), Kotane, Marks, Mofutsanyana (who was selected in mid-1932 to go on a two-and-a-half-year sojourn), and Josie.[11]

The Soviet Union's attacks on racism, racial injustice, and the capitalist exploitation of non-Europeans in South Africa resonated with black party members, who saw making a pilgrimage to the "Red Mecca" as a life-changing opportunity. However, training at KUTV was not about catering to student idealism but giving party members a "theoretical and practical knowledge of revolutionary struggle."[12] They took general education courses along with a rigorous dose of courses specifically designed for party cadres: Political Economy, History of the Revolutionary Movement and the Comintern, Historical Materialism and Lenin___, Military Science, and Party and Trade Union Building. They were also given opportunities for practical experience, such as working on a collective, operating in an underground, and military training.

While in Moscow, Mofutsanyana came to realize that ordinary Russians on the street perceived him and other black students as oddities. Children would point at him and shout out, "Come see the Negro!" He and other black students were also disturbed by the racism they experienced in the Soviet Union. They complained about one play, *The Negro Child and the Ape,* in which black people were disparagingly portrayed. They sent a resolution to the Comintern expressing their concerns, which officials did not really address since, according to communist doctrine, racism could not exist in the Soviet Union.[13]

While Edwin was in Moscow, he learned that Josie had an affair with Moses Kotane and had given birth to a baby boy, Dennis.[14] He was upset by this news, but he kept in mind the counsel of Eugene Dennis, the Comintern representative in South Africa in 1932 and 1933, who told him that there were situations in which revolutionaries had to cope with personal setbacks and maintain their devotion to the struggle. However, after his return to Johannesburg in August or September 1934, his relationship with Josie deteriorated.

For African communists like Josie, the Russian Revolution of 1917 "offered a vision of the world in which working and oppressed people would cast off the yoke of oppression and take control of their own destinies.[15]" She consistently praised the Soviet Union for its accomplishments. As the CPSA was celebrating the fifteenth anniversary of the revolution, she addressed a series of meetings in its honor. At the Trades Hall on November 7, 1932, she applauded the revolution's achievements:

> What the workers of Russia had done was a lesson to every worker irrespective of colour. She said she knew that it was hard for the black workers of South Africa to realize that they could win freedom in the same way as the Russian people had done but I can tell you that it is just as easy for you as it was for the Russian people. You might say they were not oppressed in the same way you are, but they were, and what they have done, if you do [it, it] will make you free people.[16]

After returning from her year in Moscow, she again praised the Soviet Union, touting its achievements in advancing women's rights and for being "the only country in the world where women have full equality, not merely in constitutional law, in family law, but in all spheres of social life."[17]

Thus, it was not surprising that after Edwin returned home, she wasted no time in lobbying to be sent to Moscow. She criticized party leaders who had gone to Moscow for training for not identifying others to go there so that the party could nurture future leaders, and she had to overcome the opposition of Edwin, who wanted to send another woman, a "Comrade Jane," instead.[18] According to Josie, Jane could not read or write English and would have had to take English language classes once she arrived in Moscow. Edwin likely did not support Josie because Dennis had been born shortly after his return, and he insisted on her taking primary responsibility for the child. However, Josie dealt with that issue by calling on her stepmother, Clara Emma, to take care of Dennis at her home at Robinson Deep Mine and her grandmother to look after the older children in their Sophiatown home. Josie's efforts were ultimately successful, and in mid-1935 she became the first party member to go to the Soviet Union for study since Edwin's return.

Those who went to the Soviet Union were very creative about assuming new identities or coming up with justifications for their need to travel. Passport controls for South Africans entering and leaving the country were lax. Even though he could not drive, Moses Kotane had taken the identity of a driver, Kumalo, and made his way by boat to London and eventually St. Petersburg.[19] Nzula had used the passport of Conan Doyle Modiakgotla, a musician who had been an officer in a CPSA affiliate, the League of African Rights. Nzula had assumed Modiakgolta's identity and posed as a member of Griffiths Motsieloa's well-known singing group, which was heading to London to make records.

Mofutsanyana had exited by inserting his photo into the passport of a white comrade, Eddie Roux, when he crossed into Mozambique.

Josie's ruse was that she was a nurse attendant accompanying Mrs. Matilda First, who was awarded a trip to Yalta as a reward for her family's contributions to the CPSA. Mrs. First would be checking into a sanitorium in the Soviet Union.[20] Despite being owners of the Union Mattress Company, Matilda and her husband, Julius, were party members who donated generously to it.[21] Josie, however, was certain that their travel plans had become known to others. On the day she and Mrs. First left the mattress company for their trip, an office worker had "shouted at me that I am going to Russia. When I tried to explain to her, she shouted don't bluff us we know that Mrs. First is going to Russia and taking you with her." At the Johannesburg train station, several male employees of the Firsts' company showed up and peered suspiciously into the windows of train compartments.[22] In Cape Town a "comrade" of the Jewish Worker's Club saw them off at the dock, a sure sign that they were making their way to the Soviet Union.

Upon reaching the Soviet Union, students were sworn to a strict code of secrecy and had to hand in all their travel documents and passports. Students were instructed to refrain from "casual conversations with outsiders," from revealing where they came from or why they were in the Soviet Union, and from meeting with "unknown foreigners." They could not appear in photos or use their real names while they were in the Soviet Union.[23] Hence, Josie operated under the name Beatrice Henderson.[24]

In her year at KUTV she suffered a series of illnesses. Soon after arriving in Moscow in mid-1935, she was struck with acute appendicitis and had to have an operation.[25] In Moscow's extremely cold winter, she repeatedly contracted bronchitis and had to be hospitalized nine times.

Throughout the rest of her life, she volunteered little to her family about her experiences in Moscow. She told her daughter Hilda that a doctor forced her to eat a quarter pound of butter daily to build up her resistance to the frigid temperatures but that she never got used to it.[26] One of the few other stories Josie related was that when she walked around the streets of Moscow, Russian women would stare at her intently and cross themselves because, as she explained, they perceived her as the devil, having never seen a black woman before.

The continued infighting within the CPSA and the Stalinist purges in the Soviet Union also disrupted Josie's studies. The CPSA's ideological battles had become so disruptive that it had shrunk to a few dozen members, prompting the Comintern to call on a Frenchman, André Marty, head of the Comintern's Anglo-American Secretariat, to establish a commission to investigate and resolve the disputes. The commission invited Roux and Kotane, who supported the Native Republic slogan, to Moscow to represent one faction, but only Kotane showed up.[27] Representing the other faction were Marks and Nikin Sobia (the alias of Jack Hilton), but Sobia did not show up, and Marks made it only as far as Paris, where he surely heard the stories about purges taking place in Moscow. In December 1934, the assassination of the Leningrad party boss, Sergei Kirov, had touched off a wave of repression in which Stalin purged suspected ideological renegades, especially Trotskyites, as well as cadres charged with opposing him. Apollon Davidson and Irina Filatova speculate that Marks understood that any loser in the showdown would be caught up in the purges and probably not be allowed to return to South Africa, so he made up excuses for not attending the hearing. Maurice Richter was then delegated to represent their position. He joined Lazar Bach, who was already studying in Moscow.[28]

When the Marty Commission began holding hearings in late November 1935, the principal combatants, Kotane and Bach, faced off. Although Josie was a peripheral figure in the investigation, she was called to testify. Despite her close relationship with Kotane, she likely understood that a lot more was at stake than scoring ideological points. She could not appear to side with either faction, so she claimed that she had not engaged in any of the disputes.

Nevertheless, the commission subjected her to sharp questioning about various issues. One was a petition she had signed in Johannesburg in which Kotane called for Bach's dismissal for issuing reports inflating the number of members working in the mines. At the time, Bach had labeled her "an enemy of the people" for siding with Kotane. Josie's explanation was that she was unwell when she signed the petition and did not fully understand its contents.[29] Furthermore, she claimed that she had had little contact with Kotane after he returned from his stint in Moscow in 1933 beyond district meetings where party activities, not doctrinal questions, were discussed.[30]

To the Marty Commission her most serious offense was a speech she delivered at the Comintern's Seventh Congress (July/August 1935), a few months after she arrived in Moscow. The line the congress adopted was that with the rise of Nazi Germany, fascism was now the principal enemy and communist parties around the world were expected to form "anti-imperialist" fronts against fascism with organizations they would have previously regarded derisively as "reformist" or even enemies. In South Africa, this meant taking on an impossible task: forging unity between black and white workers.

According to Mpama, Aleksander Zusmanovich, head of the Africa Department at KUTV, and Bach had handed her a speech that she then presented "because it was given to me." Although she had some minor differences with the speech and wanted to highlight women's issues and the martyred Johannes Nkosi, Zusmanovich and Bach blocked her from adding anything. According to her, "I agreed and said nothing further, and put it like that."[31]

To the commission, the problem with the wording of her speech was that even though it followed the new Comintern line, which advocated a popular front, words had been inserted calling for the eventual creation of an "independent native republic, for the confiscation of all land and its distribution between native peasants and poor white farmers." White workers and the white poor, who had interpreted the Native Republic slogan as "a purely native slogan directed against the whites," were now "beginning to understand that the slogan of an independent native republic corresponds to their interest, that it expresses the general endeavour to take up the struggle on the part of all who are suffering under the oppression of English and Boer capitalists."[32] In other words, the popular front was a step toward the creation of a Native Republic.

Josie dug an even deeper hole for herself by expressing her skepticism to the commission that an alliance of blacks and whites in South Africa was remotely possible. She conceded that if whites were

> politically educated, there might be a possibility of a
> united front with whites but only if we knew what line
> to take. We were working blindly, and instead of making
> use of the white people we drove them away, we did not
> allow any white man to come near our meetings. Here
> is one thing we must take into consideration, there is
> no getting away from it, the white man may be very
> poor that he will be below the grade of the native, but
> he is anti-native and the same thing is with the natives.

> The natives look upon the whites as exploiters.... They
> cannot understand that there can be such white men
> who can come out in sympathy with the native workers.
> For the mere reason that his skin is white, he is looked
> upon as an exploiter of the native people.[33]

Josie told the commissioners that she did not fully understand what she had read in her speech. She explained, "I am not politically advanced, and when I want to speak in my way, I am told that is not politics; you must speak in this way." But she did not put the blame for her remarks on the others: "I made no objections when it was given to me; I accepted it.... But I take full responsibility upon myself; I was responsible for putting the speech before the Congress as it is."[34] Nevertheless, she expressed her irritation that she had been directed to deliver speeches she had not herself prepared. She had come to Moscow for political study and preparing documents but instead "found that people are treated like children."[35]

In the end Josie had to repent her failures to challenge the practices of CPSA leaders. "I just sat down and did not attempt to force the comrades to carry out the Party line." So she promised that after returning to South Africa, she planned to "show the comrades their mistakes and help them come up to our political level and struggle against imperialism."[36]

In his defense, Zusmanovich claimed that he and Bach had gone over the speech with her twenty times to make sure they were all in agreement and to clarify issues, but they had failed to understand that any mention of the Native Republic was now heresy. However, the commission held Zusmanovich and Bach, not Josie, accountable for her words.

At the hearing's conclusion, the commission did not side with either Kotane or Bach. But it did permit Kotane to return to South Africa on the understanding that he would not accept a leadership position in the CPSA and that he would stay out of factional fighting and make way for new leaders who were untainted by the controversies. Although the commission dismissed Zusmanovich from his position at KUTV, its primary scapegoat was Bach, who was instructed to stay in Moscow and assist with the commission's work.[37]

In late 1936, Stalin began unleashing unleashed a coordinated campaign of mass terror against anyone believed to be an "enemy of the state." Anyone, even the most ardent communist, could be attacked as a fifth columnist, a spy, or a saboteur. Hence, not only ordinary citizens but also commissars, politburo members, army officers, Bolsheviks who had been in the 1917 revolution, scientists, artists, and even the dreaded secret police were subject to arrest. By the time the Great Terror wound down in 1938, an estimated two million people had been arrested, seven hundred thousand executed, and 1.3 million consigned to labor camps.[38]

Foreign communists, especially political refugees living in the Soviet Union, were singled out, and the Comintern was vilified as a "nest of spies." As a result, the Comintern, most of whose six hundred officials were foreign born, was gutted.[39] The historian Karl Schlogel explains, "As Comintern people they were at home all over the world, had connections everywhere, and were therefore ideal candidates to be accused of running a network of international plots and conspiracies."[40]

Bach and the Richter brothers, Maurice and Paul, were also victims. First, they were expelled from the CPSA. Then Bach was charged with having participated "in factional work in the Communist Party in South Africa" and coming "into contact [in the Soviet Union] with elements undeserving of confidence and to having hidden the fact from the Party." The Richters were accused of moving "in circles hostile to the Party and to the Soviet government." After additional evidence was offered that Bach and the Richters were consorting with Trotskyites engaged in antigovernment activity, the Comintern executive concluded they had gone further than just involvement in antiparty activity and were participating in "criminal activity." Although the Comintern went no further than that, on March 10, 1937, the Richters and Bach were arrested. The Richters were executed a year later, while Bach was sent to a concentration camp in the eastern Soviet Union, where he died in February 1941.[41]

Return to South Africa

In mid-1936, as Josie prepared for her return to South Africa, her suspicion grew that her cover had been blown. At the Lux Hotel, while she was packing books to send to South Africa, she asked Comintern representative Eugene Dennis about where he was sending them. When he told her he would be mailing them to the Union Mattress Company, she advised him that that was a risky address because she had left South Africa as Mrs. First's nurse and mailing the books to the factory would be a sure tip-off to the police about where she had been, as she had left no definite address.

Josie also suspected she was being watched—by whom she was not sure. One evening while she and Dennis were waiting for Zusmanovich to show up at the Lux, she noticed "a man in a white hat looking at me." Dennis instructed her to leave the hotel immediately by another exit. She identified the man as "Meyerson," but it is unclear from her account whether she suspected him of being an informer or whether he was someone who was not supposed to know she was there, for security reasons.[42]

Josie's concerns about informers were well-founded because her speech to the Seventh Congress had been brought to the attention of British intelligence, which passed the information on to the South African Police. South African officials, tipped off that she and Bach were traveling back to South Africa on forged passports, alerted harbor officials to be on the lookout for them in November 1936.[43] We do not know exactly how Josie returned home, but a photograph of her taken in Mozambique shows that it was one of her stopovers in 1936 and that she probably reentered South Africa from there.

Figure 3.1. Josie Mpama/Palmer in Mozambique on her return from the Soviet Union. (Hilda Johnson)

4

Declarations of Independence

During the 1930s, the turmoil within the CPSA over ideological disputes consumed and almost destroyed it. In Johannesburg and Moscow, Josie was fully engaged in the conflicts that plagued the party, including a radical proposal by Edwin Mofutsanyana in 1938 to divide the party into black and white wings. Sometimes she followed the party line, but she was not reticent about staking out independent positions and sharply criticizing CPSA policies that she believed were not rooted in South African realities.

Through the party, she was active on both national and local fronts and participated in the All-African Convention, the Non-European Unity Front, and the African National Congress.

Josie was outspoken on gender issues and critiqued the sexism that was rampant among both black and white men that marginalized women. Her views evolved on African women and men working together. Initially she supported women working cooperatively with men, but in the 1940s she shifted her stance to backing the creation of separate organizations for women.

She also spelled out her thinking on how to engage black women in protests through pressing issues such as supporting the home brewing of beer and opposing police raids, high bus fares, expensive rent and housing, expulsions from black locations, and pass laws that affected their daily lives as individuals and their families and communities.

In 1947, she took a significant step as one of the founders of the Transvaal All-Women's Union, which included women from all racial groups and prefigured the formation of the Federation of South African Women in 1954.

Sophiatown

Returning from her year in the Soviet Union, Josie rejoined Edwin Mofutsanyana and their four children in Sophiatown, where they had been residing since 1931 at the home of her grandmother, Johanna Garson, at 31 Bertha Street. A midwife, Johanna occupied the front part of the house, while Josie's family lived in a cottage in the backyard that Johanna normally let out to renters. This was their residence until 1939, when Josie and her children moved to 60 Edith Street.[1]

Government policy on Africans living in cities followed the Stallard principle—that they were there to serve whites and that where they lived should be tightly restricted.[2] In contrast to municipal townships, Sophiatown was a haven for blacks because they did not need official permission to reside there, and so they could

Figure 4.1. Grandmother Garson at Sophiatown home.
(Palmer family album)

not be arbitrarily expelled. Four-and-a-half miles from downtown Johannesburg, Sophiatown had originally been planned for whites, but after a sewage disposal plant was built next to it, few whites took up residence. After World War I, newly urbanized Africans, Coloureds, and Indians, attracted by the freehold plots of land and the absence of direct administrative oversight by intrusive white superintendents that was typically found in black locations, began moving in in large numbers.[3]

There was little accommodation for newly arrived black people in Johannesburg, so white landlords—who owned about 80 percent of the land in Sophiatown—maximized their income for paying off mortgage bonds by renting shacks at exorbitant rates in their backyards and cramming in as many people as possible. A handful of black professionals owned property and built impressive homes. One was Dr. A. B. Xuma, the sole Western-trained African doctor in Johannesburg, who lived at 85 Toby Street in an eight-room brick home with two garages. However, for the vast majority of the roughly twelve thousand people who were packed into Sophiatown by the late 1930s, finding space in a corrugated iron shack in a backyard was their only option. What made Sophiatown distinct, according to Xuma's biographer Steven Gish, was "the fact that property owners and tenants, educated and educated, Africans, and those of different races, lived side by side.[4]

The struggle to pay high rents was the issue that Josie commented on in her first published newspaper piece in 1933.[5] Sophiatown landlords knew that under the Urban Areas Act renters could be easily expelled from urban areas if they lived in nonfreehold locations, so they deliberately increased rents. Residents had the choice of leaving Sophiatown and risking being expelled from town or staying and refusing to pay the high rents. Those who chose the latter often were evicted.[6] Josie called on black women in particular to "demand to live where you choose and demand that your landlord reduce your rent again in those cases where it has been raised. You must help to build the future of your children who are starving. Many of these children may be seen prowling round the market trying to pick rotten fruit and vegetables for food."[7]

Despite its potholed streets, absence of streetlights, poor sanitation, limited water taps, and cramped living spaces, Sophiatown developed a strong identity with a vibrant and resilient community life. It was different from other African locations in the Johannesburg area because it was home to a mélange of racial and ethnic groups—Africans, Coloureds, Indians, Chinese, and even a handful of whites. Indians, Coloureds, and Chinese owned shops. Churches and schools abounded. It attracted a remarkable mix of people—politicians of all stripes, writers, musicians, teachers, clergy, shopkeepers, doctors, and shebeen operators.[8]

Sophiatown was a cultural hub for musicians who nurtured jazz, blues, and an urban black blend called *marabi* and who performed at theaters such as the

Picture Palace and the Odin Cinema, jazz clubs, and dance parties in backyard shebeens. The CPSA sponsored some of the concerts and dances.[9] It was also a hotbed of gang activity. Gangs such as the Americans, the Russians, the Vultures, the Berliners, and the Gestapo performed their specializations—extortion, pickpocketing, protection rackets, gambling, bootleg liquor, robbery of railway cars—sometimes in Sophiatown but mainly around the region. Known for their stylish clothes, these *tsotsis* (urban criminals) created a street patois, *tsotsitaal.*[10]

Don Mattera, who was a leader of the Vultures as a teen, described Sophiatown this way: "It was a dog-eat-dog world, harsh and yet tender in a strange, paradoxical way."[11] To the con man Dugmore Boetie, Sophiatown was "the skeleton with the permanent grin. A live carcass bloated with grief and happiness. Where decency was found in filth and beauty hidden behind ugliness. Where vice was a virtue and virtue a vice."[12]

Like for most Sophiatown residents, making ends meet was a constant struggle for Josie and Edwin because they did not receive regular salaries as party functionaries until the late 1930s. A handful of African women with education could find jobs as nurses and teachers, but most women lived precarious existences and generated income in the informal sector as beer brewers, dressmakers, food hawkers, prostitutes, and domestic servants and laundresses for white households, for which it was cheaper to have black women do their washing rather than an established laundry. The journalist Jameson Coka described the latter's plight: "Every hour of the day they are seen with huge bundles of dirty linen from town and as often with big bundles of clean and ironed clothes. Women of all ages, young girls, hardly in their teens and old matrons all carry the eternal washing."[13] Although laundresses had to provide their own soap, water, coal, wood, and fares for transport, they had greater independence because they could work from their homes while looking after their children.

Josie and her children generated income by doing laundry for white families. This was work she had been exposed to as a child, and as for other laundresses it suited her needs because she could earn money while raising her young children and find time for her political activism. Her daughter Carol remembered the children being trained at an early age to wash and iron clothes, which they picked up twice a week from white families. Their routine was to start with handkerchiefs, then napkins, and finally tea towels. Carol stood on a vegetable box while she ironed. When she reached high school, she graduated to shirts. At Christmas and Easter, they sewed children's clothes for white families. Carol operated a Singer sewing machine with a crank handle, while Josie helped with hemming.

Because Josie and Edwin were so devoted to party activities, their children ran the household. As Josie told them, they were "practicing for being responsible." The

Figure 4.2. Josie Mpama/Palmer with her children in the 1940s. *Bottom row:* Josie, Dennis, and Hilda. *Top row:* Francis and Carol. (Hilda Johnson)

rule was that half of everything they earned had to go to maintaining the home.[14] To bring in more money, Josie and Edwin even occasionally played *fah fee,* the Chinese numbers game.

While Josie's family was in Sophiatown, its name, Mpama, was anglicized to Palmer. Johanna made the decision to make it easier to enroll the children at a Coloured school in Doornfontein. Josie had spoken Afrikaans in Potchefstroom, and she and her children spoke English and Afrikaans in Sophiatown. It was only when she moved to Mzimhlophe in Soweto in the late 1940s that she started picking up African languages. In a public speech in 1936, she admitted her inability to speak an African language: "My people I am sorry that I cannot address you in any vernacular language because

Figure 4.3. Josie (*sitting*) appearing in a play put on by the Bantu People's Theatre. (Palmer family album)

we people who *grow* up in Johannesburg have to take up a foreign language."[15]

One of Josie's leisure activities was performing in a drama group called the Bantu People's Theatre, which aimed to reflect "the true life, feelings, struggles and aspirations of the Bantu people." Among the plays they put on were Eugene O'Neill's *The Hairy Ape* and *Plumes* and *Recruiter* by African American playwrights affiliated with the International Youth League.[16] For one play on African American life in the nineteenth century staged at Undermoon Hall in Sophiatown, the actors strove to approximate African American speech, which was described as "a sort of broken English." A review in the *Bantu World* advised them "to adhere to the original texts as much as possible."[17]

Black and White Reds

Throughout the 1930s and 1940s, Josie remained a party loyalist, but comments she made in Moscow and her columns in the party newspaper *Umsebenzi* demonstrated her practical concerns that the CPSA had to be rooted in the realities of South Africa as distinct from Europe and that it had to explain its policies in terms and language that appealed to black people. She was not reluctant to express independent views that reflected her own experiences on a range of issues: party members' attitudes toward organized religion, the party's shrinking membership, and *Umsebenzi*'s content. She asked challenging questions about why party membership had dwindled to a handful of die-hards and why the party, despite its reputation for being a multiracial organization, had failed at broadening its appeal beyond its white following—largely Eastern European Jewish immigrants—who were very influential in party affairs.

She criticized the dismissive manner many party members had toward black Christians. Although she had dropped out of the church when she became a member of the party, she applied the lessons from her involvement in the Methodist Church and the Potchefstroom protests. Because she was aware of the limits of party ideology in attracting and retaining new African members, she was acutely sensitive to her comrades' inability to deal with people who had deeply held religious beliefs.

Josie related her attempt to recruit into trade unions several of her church-going nephews who were prepared to work for better conditions for workers. However, Peter Ramutla, a party organizer, alienated them by bluntly telling them that "we have no place for christians [*sic*] in our ranks." Party speakers "denouncing god [*sic*]" at public meetings also turned them off:

> There is no doubt that the African people are very religious and we should organise them only around their daily grievances and daily demands, and later point out to them the role the ministers play, and only then can we win them over and in the groups the question of god can be discussed politically. This has been witnessed so many times that going or coming from church Africans stop at our meetings. They agree when they hear of their grievances and daily demands, but as soon as a speaker tells them that there is no god or use abusive language against god, they walk away and in their personal talk they admit that we are fighting to better their conditions but they refuse to work with us because we are against god.[18]

At party meetings, she related, members agreed with her line of argument, but when they were in public, they reverted to attacking Christians. She finally brought the issue before the party district committee, which adopted the line that communist speakers should attack clergymen in public but only raise the question of God's existence in private settings.

Issy Wolfson endorsed Josie's perspective in a report he prepared for the Comintern on conditions in South

Africa. He acknowledged that party candidates such as Mofutsanyana had been victims of their antichurch propaganda during the elections in 1937 for the Native Representative Council, when their opponents charged them with burning churches and attacking the authority of chiefs. Many Africans were also turned off when party members called intellectuals "good boys" and "agents of British imperialism."[19]

Nevertheless, Josie supported giving a different kind of religious education to women, who made up the majority of church members. The message they received in churches was that God would judge whites one day for their oppression of black people. Her view was that black people had to "wake up and demand that freedom" now because waiting for doomsday for God to intervene would not bring about change.[20]

Josie was also frustrated by the way the party ran *Umsebenzi*. According to her, the editors, especially Eddie Roux, did not encourage workers to submit articles. There was a pecking order of who could be published and who would not even be considered: "You are in the country districts; workers are in the towns and they would write, but, because an article is not well polished, or written by a Marxist-Leninist student they will throw it into the waste basket."[21] After she arrived in Moscow, she observed that Comintern officials were not well versed in struggles taking place throughout South Africa because they were not covered in *Umsebenzi*. She had submitted an article to the paper before she left

South Africa but doubted it had been published because of her weak command of English and poor writing style. "If anything was wrong with the article," she complained, "could it not have been corrected and put in?"[22]

Josie related that people complained that *Umsebenzi* no longer commented on worker news and that its level of language was too difficult for the common person to understand. "When we go with 'Umsebenzi' [to the black townships], the workers ask: what paper is it? And then they say, there is nothing for us in the paper: only long articles about the Soviet Union. The workers do not claim it as their paper." Instead, people were turning to "reformist" black newspapers such as *Umteteli wa Bantu, Bantu World,* and *Mochochonono* for coverage of everyday news, social life, and sports. "Our comrades do not want to own up that these papers have a big influence and are sold at a wink of an eye, because they have news."[23] Rather than providing an outlet for people to express their grievances, *Umsebenzi* was fixated on ideological issues. "The Party shouts: come to us," she charged, but the party "refused to go down to the masses."[24]

Josie was not alone in her criticism of *Umsebenzi*. Kotane noted that when the party expelled Sidney Bunting, Eugene Dennis opposed resuming its publication because the paper was associated with him. However, eight thousand copies were still printed up and, along with many pamphlets, lay in stacks in the party's main office.

Kotane also had a problem with the paper's language because it contained "long articles, long phrases which meant nothing." He compared it to *Imprecor,* the Comintern's international press publication. "If a paper is to be a mass organ for uneducated people," he advised, "it must be written so we can understand." Long essays in English were devoted to issues such as Bunting joining forces with Leon Trotsky and lengthy submissions from the Comintern, but none of them were translated into African languages. He asked, "Who can read it among the native people? They do not know who Trotsky is." Hence, "the paper was not read, there were no returns; it was simply printed, and then irregularly, sometimes once a month or once in two months."

Kotane added that the paper revived somewhat when it began including articles in African languages and readable English. Moreover, Jewish donors began contributing to the paper when it started to run articles on Adolf Hitler's rise to power. However, by 1937, the financing of the newspaper was so precarious that publication had to be suspended for six months.

Despite Josie's criticisms, she lent her support to keeping the party alive, even though by 1937 the party was virtually moribund because of its internecine battles. Membership had dropped to about fifty nationwide, and virtually the only African members in Johannesburg were the paid functionaries—Kotane, Mofutsanyana, Thibedi, Josie, and an unnamed official in the Mine Workers' Union—who were supposed to receive thirty shillings per week but often were not.[25] At the center of internal debates were two critical issues that would shape the party for many years: whether to keep the central office of the party in Johannesburg or move it to Cape Town and whether to split the party into black and white wings.

The latter proposal was controversial, to say the least. One of the enduring images of the party is that it was the only South African political organization in which blacks and whites worked comfortably together. Ray Edwards, the mother of Albie Sachs, remembered a story that symbolized the warm relations between black and white members.[26] On a bitterly cold winter evening, she and Josie, who was carrying her infant son, were recruiting new party members at Crown Mines. Sharing a pair of mittens, they each wore one at a time. However amicable the personal relationships between black and white party members could be, it was challenging to build a genuinely multiracial organization, and they had to face up to the reality that in South Africa it was extremely difficult to promote genuine organizing that crossed the color line.

CPSA records amply reveal the frictions between black and white members that had been building since the late 1920s. The issue came to a head at a central committee meeting in Johannesburg in late 1938 that was assessing party work. Mofutsanyana, chosen as general secretary of the party in 1937, questioned how realistic it was for blacks and whites to maintain a unified party and proposed splitting it into black and white wings. In his "Report on the Struggle of Africans," he produced a litany of charges about how black and white members received different treatment. He questioned how much the party was doing to raise the consciousness of Africans and whether the party was allocating enough resources for its work in the African community.[27] He charged that money was found to print leaflets for distribution among Europeans but that it was not forthcoming for African-focused materials. He criticized the suggestion of some leading white party members that salaries of party functionaries—most of whom were black—be done away with. He noted that *Umsebenzi* was no longer being published. He reported that in joint meetings of black and white members in Johannesburg, white members' reports on developments in Europe, such as the Munich Agreement of September 30, 1938, went over the heads of many blacks, who wanted to discuss how to combat oppression in their own country. As a result, they soon lost interest and did not show up again. To him, all these developments were indicators of the party's "denial of the role of the Africans in the struggle for emancipation."

Mofutsanyana's solution was for the party to split into two sections, one white and one black, "with the Executive Committee as a connecting link between the two." The reality, he contended, was that two sections were already in existence. Rather than weakening the party, creating two wings would strengthen it because the African section would then become more independent and develop ownership of the party:

> The African section of our Party which has a very low political level leans too much on the Europeans and thus has less responsibility. They do not feel that the Party is their own; they usually regard themselves as servants and tools of the Europeans. These are facts which must be faced when discussing this question irrespective of how bitter they may be.[28]

Most blacks at the meeting shared Mofutsanyana's description of the racial divide in the party. Josie agreed that white members did not have first-hand knowledge of how blacks lived or what the party was doing in the locations. If that was the case, she said, "How can they speak about these matters? Comrades must come among the masses." When Africans and whites met together, she observed, Africans were reluctant to join in discussions. But "when European comrades are absent the Natives discuss." She recommended that white party members not be involved in organizing in the African locations.

Kotane bluntly acknowledged that white members did not understand their African comrades. "We are bad psychologists," he admitted. White members had to sensitize themselves to issues that concerned black members. In general, white members knew that black members lived in locations and carried passes, but they had little first-hand knowledge of how they actually lived. Moreover, black members believed that white members controlled party finances and allocated the money for their own ends.[29]

While Kotane and Josie agreed with Mofutsanyana on the deficiencies of the party, they both opposed the idea that the party should be split into sections based on race. Kotane stated that if that happened, he would leave the party and join another organization. Whites had historically used divide-and-rule tactics to split blacks and maintain power, but

> here there is a Party which preaches equality. If we have two sections what will the psychological reaction be? It will put us back 300 or 500 years. I can join the African National Congress, the I.C.U. or any other organisation, but I will have no connection with a half-and-half organisation. What of the equality within the Party?

As Nikin Sobia put it, "If we tolerate having two sections, it is no longer a working class Party."

Kotane also introduced a resolution to move the Political Bureau from Johannesburg to Cape Town. His position was that the party had to develop a solid organizational foundation before it could move into action, but the factional disputes over ideology in the party had overshadowed it. The dysfunctionality of the central office in Johannesburg crippled activities in the rest of the country—and all the hard work Kotane had devoted to establishing committees in small towns around the country had gone for naught because general secretaries such as Marks and Mofutsanyana had been distracted by disputes and were not running the office efficiently. Kotane argued that since the members in Cape Town were working well together, the Political Bureau should be transferred to Cape Town until Johannesburg got its act together. He recognized that even though Johannesburg was still the center of the country, it could not perform that role for the time being.

No record exists of the vote on Mofutsanyana's proposal to split the party into two wings, but the decision to move the Political Bureau to Cape Town passed narrowly by six to five, with two abstentions. Although Josie was critical of Mofutsanyana's leadership of the party, she was not on the Executive Committee and likely did not vote on the resolution. As for Mofutsanyana, he shouldered the blame for the state of the party, but he was clearly fed up: "I do not care if I remain [as general secretary] or not."

The meeting's decision to move to Cape Town was fortuitous for the party because it gave it much-needed breathing space and allowed it to maintain a presence in national politics. The party also could operate without the interference of a Comintern crippled by the Great Terror in the Soviet Union.

The Party and Black Politics

However independent Josie was on party issues, she adhered to the party line when it came to its relations with black political organizations. After her return from Moscow, the party, following the Comintern's Popular Front policy instructing communist parties around the world to work with "reformist" organizations, directed her, Mofutsanyana, Kotane, and John Gomas to serve as delegates to the AAC in 1936. The AAC had been established in 1935 to respond to the controversial Hertzog bills in Parliament, which aimed to do away with the qualified African franchise in the Cape Province and to reconfigure land segregation. The 1910 constitution of the Union of South Africa, the predecessor of the Republic of South Africa, included protected clauses that required a two-third's majority in a joint session of Parliament to overturn them. Prime Minister J. B. M. Hertzog, who had been trying to get rid of the African franchise since 1926, was not able to muster enough votes until his National Party merged with Jan Smuts's South Africa Party to form the United Party in 1934.

The specter of losing the qualified Cape franchise galvanized African opinion. In December 1935, four hundred delegates from around the country converged on Bloemfontein to found the AAC to combat the Hertzog bills. At the time, the ANC was on the brink of collapsing under Pixley Seme's lackluster presidency, and it looked as if the AAC would supplant the ANC as the leading organization in the African community.[30]

Josie and other communists worked within AAC structures. Initially touting the AAC as "the mightiest movement which will shock the ruling class," she contended that since the AAC had forced the Hertzog government to make a compromise on the Native bills, the CPSA "must work in the Convention and build it up."[31] However, after some exposure to how the AAC operated, she and other communists discontinued their support for it because they believed it had poor leaders who were not prepared to provide a long-term commitment. Indeed, in 1937, she, Mofutsanyana, and others redirected their energies to begin resurrecting the ANC.

Josie was active in establishing the CPSA in Sophiatown. In 1935, she and other members opened a night school that not only introduced prospective members to political training and communist ideas but also taught practical subjects such as English and math.

Often called on to speak in black townships on community issues, Josie addressed a meeting at Western Native Township on Dingaan's Day, December 16, 1936:

> We meet on this day of the anniversary of the day on which our people were conquered by the Imperialists of this country, but we know that they fought bravely against the Dutch who were using the best weapons of the time. There is only one thing for us to do—we must unite and fight for better wages. Many things are facing the African people; the first is that we receive such low wages that we fail to educate our children. All we work for is rent and poor food, and cannot even buy clothes. From our small wages we are also forced to pay taxes, while the Europeans are taxed according

to their earnings; we should fight against this, for better wages, and against the high rents. I hope that from to-day onwards we will fight for these things and also for freedom.[32]

Josie addressed another meeting in Western Native Township on January 12, 1937, where she highlighted the high rents and paltry wages that burdened Africans. She called on Africans, Indians, and Coloureds to work together to fight against the high rents that were forcing them out of towns: "Some time back the coloured people said the native people should leave the towns because they were stinky, but to-day as they have nowhere to go to they need our whole support. We must come together and fight for our rights."[33]

In the late 1930s, she also participated in the Non-European Unity Front as assistant secretary of its Johannesburg branch. Founded in Cape Town in 1938, the NEUF had close ties to the CPSA. In the Western Cape its membership was largely made up of Coloured professionals, but around Johannesburg it reached out to Indians, Coloureds, and Africans, and its public meetings made a point of featuring speakers from all these racial groups.[34] Its primary focus was residential segregation, but Josie used the organization to speak out on issues important to her. At a meeting in Johannesburg chaired by an Anglican priest of Indian descent, Rev. Bernard Sigamoney, she referred to a report in the *Sunday Express* (June 9, 1939) that African women were

leaving their rural homes for the urban areas and becoming involved in get-rich-quick occupations such as
beer brewing and prostitution. She disagreed with the
newspaper's fear that Johannesburg was turning into
the "District Six of South Africa, and a danger to European society."[35]

In June 1939, she addressed a NEUF meeting at
New Market Square, where she shared a platform with
Dr. Yusuf Dadoo of the South African Indian Congress
and Reverend Sigamoney. She responded to those who
were skeptical of the NEUF, making an appeal that
"non-European groups" should aim for unity through
the NEUF in the same way that the main white political
parties had "sunk their differences" to form the United
Party. She also directed blacks to reach out and educate
their communities on pressing issues:

> Go into the mines, tell these people that they are
> responsible for the mining of the rich ores of this
> country in order that the others may live a rich and
> prosperous life. There is no reason why they should
> not demand higher wages which will enable them to
> live decent and respectable lives. Go into the factories,
> go on the lands, and wherever the non-European is
> working for the benefit of the employers, tell them
> that they have a right to a share and that we have a
> right to a share of the profits of the wealth of South
> Africa.
>
> We want indiscriminate [*sic*] education for our
> children, so that they may be sufficiently trained to

take up positions in the civil service, on the trams
and buses, in your big business establishments, and in
every progressive capacity. Let us demand the right of
facilitation to these opportunities and show the whites
of South Africa that we can prove ourselves equally
capable of taking our place in the civilized life of the
country, if given the chance. . . .

Let us force the Government to do away with
these passes that are forced around our necks like dog
licences. Yes, the Africans have the right to move freely
on the soil of your fatherland. . . .

You are not inferior to anybody, for you are
endowed with the same capabilities as the next man; let
the white folk give us a chance and we'll show them.[36]

For many black people, finding a secure place to
live was a constant battle, and Josie took up the cause of
people being expelled from their homes. After learning
that people were being tossed out of their homes during
a winter in the late 1930s in Bertrams, a Johannesburg
neighborhood near Doornfontein, she formed a group
to help them. They marched with evicted people to the
police headquarters at Marshall Square

and persuaded the police to let them sleep in the
cells for the night, as it was too cold for any human
being to be left sleeping in the open. The next day we
marched with all the people to Vrededorp, where we
persuaded a number of priests to put up tents in their
yards for the homeless people, until we could get other
accommodation for them. . . . It was quite a struggle,

117

and the priests were threatened with prosecution for
allowing the people to stay in their yards.[37]

Eventually the Johannesburg City Council relented and
set up temporary shelters in Noordgesig, a Coloured
township.

Josie also became involved in Alexandra, a black
township located about ten miles north of Johannesburg's city center. A freehold township like Sophiatown,
Alexandra afforded its residents a measure of relief from
municipal and urban influx controls. Africans expelled
from other urban slums or migrating in from the countryside desperately seeking work moved into Alexandra
in the thousands in the 1930s because the township was
unregulated. However, Johannesburg's white suburbs
were expanding northward at the same time, and many
Johannesburg whites, viewing Alexandra as prime land
for themselves, sought on numerous occasions to get
rid of it.[38] They depicted Alexandra as a den of vice, a
breeding ground for disease, and a haven for criminals
preying on white homes. They even attacked Alexandra's standholders as slumlords for exploiting renters.
A speaker at a meeting of Johannesburg whites in May
1939 "described Alexandra Township as the greatest
curse to natives and Europeans alike in the whole of the
Union." The meeting appealed to the mayor and the city
council to abolish Alexandra.[39]

That same month, the CPSA's Youth League organized a meeting that many Alexandra organizations

attended to protest the threat of moving residents to municipal townships. Josie joined a delegation to the mayor of Johannesburg to express the NEUF's opposition to the planned destruction of Alexandra because of its threat to sanitation and health.[40] After the mayor told the delegation that the plans were on hold pending investigations that were underway, she questioned how the city council expected to deal with the sanitation issue:

> We are quite aware of the health danger and the alarmingly high death rate now prevalent in the townships, but the removal of townships was not going to solve the problem. . . . These unpleasant conditions are due to the low economic level of the people. No matter how many times townships were going to be removed, it will not be until better living conditions were assured, with more nourishing food and better homes, that the Council can ever hope to combat the health evil. We have [had] about enough of the so many unfilled promises made by the Council from time to time, and we are no more prepared to be moved from their present abodes unless the Council could grant them loans which would enable them to build decent homes. Only under such circumstances would they be prepared to assist the Council in bettering the present conditions. They were already in league with the health committee in an attempt to combat the health danger. They would like to make

it clear to the Council that the non-Europeans were
fully aware that they were indirectly forced out of
their private properties so as to be subjected to council
area regulations. They were, therefore, only prepared
to move from the present area by the assurance of
written documents from the Council to the effect that
the houses they are asked to move into are on sale on
conditions of hire-purchase.[41]

The mayor assured the delegation that no force would
be used to move residents, but that would not be the last
time the city council tried to remove Alexandra.[42]

Rising bus fares were another grievance of Alexandra residents because they depended on cheap
transportation to get to jobs in white areas. In mid-1939,
Josie participated in a delegation comprising Constan-
tine Ramohanoe, Gaur Radebe, Gana Makabeni, and
Mofutsanyana, which met with the transport board of
the city council to present the grievances of African pas-
sengers on public transport.[43] This was a prelude to bus
boycotts organized by residents outraged by sharp in-
creases in bus fares in late 1940 and again in 1943.

On the Soviet Union, Josie followed CPSA and Comintern orthodoxies. In August 1939, there was much
consternation among CPSA members when the Soviet
Union signed a nonaggression pact with Nazi Germany.
The pact was a moment of confusion for South African
communists because Stalin was making an about-face
after years of being an implacable foe of Nazi fascism.

ANNESBURG DISTRICT COMMITTEE OF THE COMMUNIST PARTY, 1945. Seated (left to right): M. Malal, M. Harmel, ...ber, D. du Plessis (Chairman), J. Palmer, H. Watts, Standing: S. Buirski, A. Fischer, I. Wolfson, R. Fleet, E. Weinberg, W. Roberts, Y. M. Dadoo. Inset: E. T. Mofutsanyana

Figure 4.4. The CPSA's Johannesburg District Committee, 1945. (*Inkululeko*, April 14, 1945)

Hence, South African communists were unclear about which line to support when World War II broke out a month later. Following direction from the Comintern, they took the position of opposing a conflict they deemed an imperialist war. At a meeting on November 21, 1939, Josie and Max Joffe delivered speeches advising the working class to think hard before they supported the British war effort.[44] However, when Germany invaded the Soviet Union in June 1941, the CPSA dramatically switched its position to support the Allied war effort as well as tone down its criticism of Jan Smuts's government. Some communists saw the somersault as hypocritical and broke with the CPSA. But most, like Josie, were unshaken.

The period of the war and the years immediately after it was one of steady party growth. Membership expanded from a handful of the faithful in the late 1930s to several thousand by the end of the 1940s. The party won many African followers through facilitating urban protests, organizing trade unions, and taking the lead in labor actions such as the 1946 African Mine Workers' Union strike. As in Potchefstroom, the party held public meetings where hundreds of people filled out membership forms. But when party members sat down and interviewed prospective members about why they wanted to join, they found that most of them were motivated by practical concerns such as wages and high bus fares and that they were not interested in the extended training that party membership entailed.[45]

Despite Josie's prominence as a member of the CPSA, reconstructing her personal and political life during this decade is extremely difficult. The rich CPSA records that have been preserved in Moscow for the 1930s are virtually nonexistent for the following decade. South African government files occasionally contain party documents, but police raids of party offices were so frequent following World War II that party leaders began destroying their documents.

Leftist newspapers such as *Inkululeko* and *The Guardian* (South Africa) provide many details of party activities during the 1940s. Although Josie was on the Johannesburg district party committee throughout the decade, the leftist press only occasionally mentioned her.

The national political campaign with which she is most identified was the antipass campaign that the party initiated. In the early 1940s, the Smuts government, needing black labor in the war effort, had relaxed enforcement of the pass laws controlling the movement of black workers in the urban areas. The Smit Commission had recommended abolishing the pass controls, and it seemed that the government would follow suit. However, in early 1943, Johannesburg municipal officials started reinforcing pass laws, arresting ten thousand Africans in April alone. Then the Smuts government followed suit and reapplied the pass laws nationally.

The party saw this as an opportunity to put itself at the forefront of escalating black protests at a time when hundreds of thousands of Africans were moving from white farms and rural reserves into urban areas and were engaging in community struggles over housing, transportation, wages, and pass controls.

Josie's vociferously attacked pass laws.[46] In June 1943, she addressed an antipass rally outside Parliament,[47] and in November she joined with party leaders such as David Bopape, Mofutsanyana, Marks, and Dadoo to establish an antipass committee in Johannesburg. Reaching out to a revitalized ANC under President A. B. Xuma, the party launched an antipass campaign with the ANC on Easter (April 9) 1944. The following month, she convened a women's antipass conference in Johannesburg to coordinate how women would fit into the national campaign.[48]

Although Xuma was not enthusiastic about working too closely with the party, the two organizations agreed to convene an antipass conference at Johannesburg's Gandhi Hall in May, which attracted 540 delegates representing 375 organizations and laid ambitious plans to collect a million signatures for petitions opposing pass laws and presenting them to Parliament in August in Cape Town.[49] Tellingly, they did not call on people to destroy or hand in their passes. Josie, who delivered a "stirring appeal to African womanhood" at the conference, was named a trustee of the Anti-Pass Council.[50]

Although the petition drive was started with great fanfare, it never really gelled. Joining Dadoo, Kotane, and R. V. Selope-Thema, Josie was the lone woman in a delegation that went to Cape Town in June 1945 to present the petitions to government officials, but Acting Prime Minister Jan Hofmeyr refused to meet them. She was one of the main speakers at a mass meeting protesting pass laws on the Parade in Cape Town.[51]

The campaign failed not only because of government opposition but also because of the organizers' lack of funds and a structure to carry out a national campaign and a strategy for mass mobilization. Josie, in typically frank fashion, pinpointed other problems. She highlighted the lack of leadership by the central working committee in Johannesburg: "But the Transvaal, which gave birth to the Campaign and should be its heart and soul, became inactive after the Conference. Badges were not sold, petitions were not signed, meetings were not held, and even the local committees went to sleep."[52] Despite the campaign's frustrating end, Josie would return to the issue of pass laws in the 1950s when the National Party regime moved to extend passes to African women.

While Josie and other CPSA leaders such as Moses Kotane and J. B. Marks worked cooperatively with senior ANC figures, they had a hostile relationship with the ANC Youth League, established in 1944, which argued that the African nationalist movement should be led by Africans and perceived the CPSA as being controlled by whites and promoting a foreign ideology. Josie was certainly dismissive of the Youth Leaguers. At a meeting at the home of Youth League founder Walter Sisulu, he remembered Josie's sarcastic take on the Youth Leaguers' audacious challenge to ANC senior leaders: "Who are these youth who are so old?"[53]

Women's Issues and Community Struggles

In letters and columns contributed to newspapers from 1933 to 1945, Josie spoke out forcefully on black women's issues, candidly discussing why black women were not more involved in political organizations and raising questions about what would motivate them to engage in political issues. Her writings delve into racial exploitation and gendered politics.[54]

Josie questioned why African women were not playing a more public role in political struggles and were consigned to performing domestic responsibilities. In a November 1933 letter to *Mochochonono,* a newspaper produced in Basutoland, she pointed out that men— even those she said were "politically advanced"—were responsible "for the backwardness of their wives, sisters and daughters."[55] She charged that men attended sporting events and political meetings without bringing their womenfolk with them. Instead, they saw women as primarily responsible for performing domestic chores, while all that men were "concerned with is to come back and find hot dinners awaiting them." The times when men and women united to combat an injustice were when an issue such as the lodgers' permits "affects the family as a whole." But as soon as the issue was no longer pressing, the women "go back home and take to their domestic spheres."

Josie saw this patriarchal dynamic at work in the CPSA. In her writings in the Soviet Union in 1935, she vented her frustration at the party's lack of interest in recruiting women. She advised male members to "realise that womens [sic] place is not only in the kitchen. Women must be brought to meetings." She added that the party in general failed to connect with women, "who are the most militant fighters." The party was not known in women's organizations, but party leaders nevertheless did not allow her to attend social gatherings to learn what women's grievances were and how best to address them. She observed that women in the center were very active and took part in all the work, speaking on platforms and involving themselves in conflicts in the locations.[56] After returning to South Africa, though, it is evident that the party did not constrain her from organizing in black townships.

Despite her frustrations with male party leaders, the party gave her more space than the ANC, which did not allow women to become members until the ANC Women's League was established in 1943.[57] The league was even then little more than an auxiliary and was not allowed to form its own branches.

Josie also expressed her feelings about men expecting her to devote time to her family responsibilities rather than party affairs. After J. B. Marks was expelled from the party in June 1937, she was placed on the Johannesburg district party committee and put in charge of women's affairs. But Issy Wolfson did not support her appointment because he believed she could not juggle her responsibilities for both the party and her children:

> I feel she is not the right person in that job. That in
> the job of D. P. C. Johannesburg we want a really first
> class man and if we can get a good comrade to take
> up that position we will be able to improve our work
> tremendously. She has domestic duties which interfere
> with her political activities, and that means she is not
> able to devote the time.[58]

But Josie stuck to her guns and remained on the district committee.

In the mid-1930s, Josie took the view that black women and men shared a common barrier, the color bar, that condemned them to a subordinate position. Thus, despite her frustrations with patriarchal controls, when it came to seeking legal and social equality and fighting against injustices, her priority for women was standing "shoulder to shoulder" with men rather than challenging gender relations or male power.

Nevertheless, she was aware that women's commitment to a specific issue depended on how it affected their daily lives. For instance, she expressed deep reservations about the support African women should give to opposing the Representation of Natives Act, one of the Hertzog bills, which proposed to do away with the qualified franchise held by some African men in the Cape Province. Because the bill did not affect African women, she maintained, they "did not think it important to assist their men to maintain the vote."[59] She wondered how hard they should work to keep a vote that benefited a small number of African men when some African men openly questioned whether African women were fit to hold the vote at all.[60]

Drawing on her experiences in Potchefstroom, she believed that the best way to mobilize women and men together was by engaging them in family and community issues. She criticized another Hertzog bill, the Natives Trust and Land Act, whose aim was to drive Africans back to the land and to control the recruitment and employment of African laborers. She suggested that women be made aware of how the bill would affect them and warned that their fathers, husbands, brothers, and sons would be driven out of the urban areas to the rural reserves and white farms. She urged women to engage with men in a joint struggle against this bill:

"We, women, should come on to the field as strugglers, for only with our help can our men fight successfully against this new bill."[61]

Over time, though, Josie came to realize that there were specific situations in which women had to act on their own. Since national organizations such as the ANC provided little space for women to advance their interests, she believed that black women would be better served by "forming separate women organizations."[62] One organization she cited was the National Council of African Women, which was established at the same time as the AAC, in 1935. However, she was very critical of the shortcomings of its leaders, whom she accused of burying it by not allowing space for other organizations.[63]

One women's organization Josie participated in was the Daughters of Africa (DOA), founded in Durban in 1932 by Lillian Tshabalala, who had spent time in the United States in the late 1920s furthering her education. Inspired by the "racial respectability" of African American women who were active in networks of social clubs, Tshabalala wanted to apply that model to African women in South Africa.[64] The DOA reached out primarily to the small group of mission-educated women who wanted to advance themselves

Josie most likely met Tshabalala when she moved to Alexandra in the late 1930s. In newspaper accounts of DOA meetings, Josie was often listed as an assistant secretary. At a meeting on December 9, 1940, attended by representatives of the six DOA branches, she served as secretary and was described as a "live wire."[65] In her 1977 interview with Julia Wells, Josie said she eventually dropped out of the DOA after a few years because it was not more directly engaged in protest politics—despite the fact that Tshabalala joined the African Democratic Party when it was established in 1943, and DOA Women's Brigades were involved in the Alexandra bus boycott of 1943.

In April 1947, women participating in an International Women's Day meeting resolved to found a "non-colour bar women's organisation." Josie was one of the speakers. The meeting led to the establishment of the multiracial Transvaal All-Women's Union, which had close ties to the CPSA. Josie was its secretary. The organization's objectives included promoting "equal rights for all South African women, protective legislation for women and children, and a commitment to join with women of other nations in a struggle for world peace against fascism and racism."[66] Although the organization did not expand beyond the Transvaal and did not follow through on its plan to organize a national meeting of women, it foreshadowed the discussions that led to the planning meeting of FEDSAW in 1953.

Addressing the question of how black women could be mobilized to act on issues concerning them, she connected with women on bread-and-butter issues that affected family and community. As someone who earned money as a laundress, she understood the vulnerability of many urban African women who struggled to make ends meet through the informal economy and protect their families. As ANC activist Maggie Resha said in her autobiography, "An eagle's nest on top of a precipice is more of a home, and more secure, than a black woman's home."[67]

Josie involved herself in what Maxine Molyneux calls "practical gender needs"—issues that addressed "everyday responsibilities" that affected women's lives.[68] Josie saw that women resisted when their livelihoods as well as their families were under assault. So, she argued that "the broad masses of women" could be mobilized in the "struggle against high rents, low wages, mass arrests and evictions, for better houses, free medical attendance, higher and better education, home brewing of beer for personal consumption and for social equality."[69]

For instance, in the African location of the East Rand city of Benoni in 1937, she backed protests against what residents perceived as a compulsory medical examination for venereal diseases. Although city officials claimed that the examination was not mandatory, residents questioned why the town council took over responsibility for the examination from the district surgeon and why the exams were to be held at the pass office.[70]

Another issue that Josie took interest in was beer brewing. In the decades following World War I, the government struggled to stem the flow of tens of thousands of black women into the urban areas because it was prohibited from using pass laws as a control measure. Instead, it tried to cut off women's independent sources of income, such as brewing beer. For many urban African women, beer brewing was vital to their families' survival since they could not solely depend on the low wages of men. And for a growing number of women who were in the cities on their own, beer brewing was one of their few sources of income.

However, white municipal officials wanted to gain complete control over beer sales in the locations. In 1937, Parliament tightened the controls over beer brewing by passing an amendment to the Urban Areas Act stipulating that municipalities could acquire a monopoly over beer brewing in the townships or allow a licensed brewer to supply beer to residents. Not surprisingly, most white officials opted for a monopoly because the sale of beer to African men produced hefty revenues (it was popularly known as "pink gold") that went directly into the Native Revenue Account, where it paid for white administration in black locations.

Attempting to control the sale of home brew, white officials unleashed police vans to pick up women brewers. "The police," Josie said, "have decided to terrify you to such an extent that instead of boycotting the canteens, which is the general feeling, you will be so scared that the canteens will be opened without the least resistance."[71] The repeated police raids led to ugly clashes and riots.[72]

Josie was a consistent defender of women beer brewers. In a report to the CPSA, she advocated launching a campaign against municipally run beer halls and for women to be allowed to brew a gallon of beer a day at their homes. She believed that this would be as popular with women elsewhere as it had been in Potchefstroom. She urged the CPSA to raise this issue in organizations women participated in, such as the Women's League of Justice and *stokvels,* where they discussed ways of generating more income. She cited the case of Bloemfontein, where women had won the right to brew a gallon of beer in their homes every month, and Potchefstroom, where women were permitted to brew a gallon of beer during the New Year's holidays.[73]

As secretary of the NEUF's Transvaal branch, Josie testified in 1941 at the "Kaffir" Beer Commission, which had been established after African leaders and some sympathetic white liberals lobbied the government to investigate the controversy. Her submission was sympathetic to home brewing for Africans living in urban areas regardless of whether they were tenants or standholders.[74] She opposed the licensing of municipally run beer canteens for Africans, reasoning that even if they were established in the locations, women still preferred to brew beer at home because African men would then be spending their money in households rather than augmenting municipal revenues. A consequence of the constant police raids was that they forced beer brewers to prepare a more potent concoction known as *skokiaan,* which could be prepared in a short time.[75] And that led to more drunkenness. Josie testified, "But if they are given the right to brew their own Kaffir beer

I am sure there would not be half the trouble that we have today."

Josie stated that the NEUF supported a dual system: establishing beer halls for men who did not have their wives with them and permitting home brewing for those who did not want to be in a place where a "respectable native" would not go to drink. The result, she said, was that "it would lower his dignity" because he was drinking with "a person with whom he does not associate." Rather, she advocated that people be given the right to "drink in the quiet of their own homes if they wish to do so." She also testified that the quantity of beer should not be limited because most people did not sell much.

Many of the issues, especially pass laws and their impact on African women, with which Josie was involved in the 1930s and 1940s, continued to demand her attention in subsequent decades. But the context for her activism changed dramatically when the United Party government of Jan Smuts lost in the 1948 general election to the National Party, which began introducing a more repressive regime driven by a comprehensive, systematic set of policies called apartheid, which intensified racial segregation and clamped down on dissidents.

5

Apartheid

A new chapter opened in Josie's life when the Afrikaner-led National Party took power in 1948 with the goal of introducing apartheid, a comprehensive program that sought to engineer profound changes in the social, political, and economic order regardless of their consequences. The National Party sought to intensify racial segregation, and within a few years Parliament passed sweeping laws that classified people into races and determined their identities, where they could live, whom they could marry and have sexual relations with, what they might be taught, what kind of work they could perform, and virtually every other aspect of social life. It also began tightening controls over migrant labor and blacks living in urban areas by imposing stricter pass laws and expelling black people from freehold townships such as Sophiatown. Colin Bundy observed, "For black South Africans, ordinary urban life was criminalised; at their peak, the Pass Laws jailed millions of Africans per decade for being in the wrong place at the wrong time, without the right papers."[1] During the 1950s, the government's move to extend the pass laws to African women was met with great resistance.

The government was obsessed with internal security and sought to quash any opposition to its plans. In the process, it turned the lives of Josie and other CPSA members upside down in a very direct way through the Suppression of Communism Act of 1950, a hallmark law that declared the CPSA illegal and allowed the government to purge communists from trade unions.[2]

The disbanding of the CPSA did not prevent Josie from remaining at the forefront of antiapartheid campaigns. She was a prominent voice opposing the extension of pass laws to black women and worked through the ANC and a newly created organization, the Federation of South African Women, until a government-issued banning order and her fragile health forced her to the sidelines in the mid-1950s.

Apartheid and the CPSA

Soon after taking the reins of power, the apartheid regime set about targeting its opponents, but none received more attention than its primary enemy, the CPSA. The Suppression of Communism Act provided for the appointment of a government "liquidator" to prepare "a list of persons who are or have been office bearers, officers, members or active supporters of the Communist Party of South Africa." Compiling evidence from security police and informers in the party about the activities of communists and their sympathizers, the liquidator amassed a list of nearly six hundred names. In Josie's case, the liquidator's office wrote to Berrange and Wasserzug,[3] the law firm representing her, and justified her listing, citing a litany of her party activities: that she had attended seventeen meetings of the party's Johannesburg district committee from April 2, 1945, to September 9, 1946, and that she had sent apologies for not attending meetings on two occasions; that she had been appointed to the party's organizing committee on April 1, 1945, and served on its municipal affairs, propaganda and education, and antipass subcommittees in 1946; and that she had attended a meeting of the party's central committee on July 5, 1945, in Cape Town, at which she was consulted about the financial standing of the party's Sophiatown branch. The liquidator, J. de V. Louw, even felt compelled to record her involvement in making "arrangements with other women party members for a midday meal to be served to certain 'accused' at the 'West Premises.'"[4]

Under the law, an individual could make a representation for why he or she should not be placed on the list. The list was the "truth commission" of its time because listed people could choose to explain their relationship to the party. Some former communists submitted impassioned letters explaining how they had broken with the party and should not be listed.[5] Even though Josie was no longer an active CPSA member when the Suppression of Communism Act was enacted, she was still

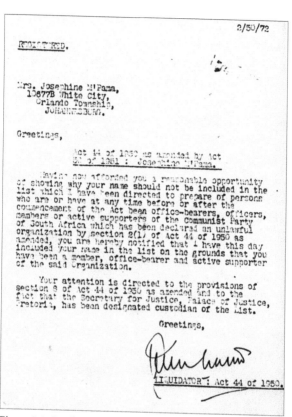

RE[...]STERED.

Mrs. Josephine M'Pama,
15677B White City,
Orlando Township,
JOHANNESBURG.

Greetings,

Act 44 of 1950 as amended by Act
50 of 1951 : Josephine M'Pama.

Having now afforded you a reasonable opportunity
of showing why your name should not be included in the
list which I have been directed to prepare of persons
who are or have at any time before or after the
commencement of the Act been office-bearers, officers,
members or active supporters of the Communist Party
of South Africa which has been declared an unlawful
organization by section 2(1) of Act 44 of 1950 as
amended, you are hereby notified that I have this day
included your name in the list on the grounds that you
have been a member, office-bearer and active supporter
of the said Organization.

Your attention is directed to the provisions of
section 8 of Act 44 of 1950 as amended and to the
fact that the Secretary for Justice, Palace of Justice,
Pretoria, has been designated custodian of the List.

Greetings,

LIQUIDATOR : Act 44 of 1950.

Figure 5.1. South African government notice listing Josephine
Mpama as a member of the Communist Party, September 15,
1950. (Josie Mpama/Palmer's banning file)

served with a notice at 6:50 a.m. on September 15, 1950,
that she had been placed on the list. After she did not
appeal her listing, the liquidator then issued her the following letter:

Having now afforded you a reasonable opportunity of showing why your name should not be included in the list which I have been directed to prepare of persons who are or who have at any time before or after the commencement of the Act been office-bearers, officers, members or active supporters of the Communist Party of South Africa which has been declared an unlawful organization by section 2(1) of Act 44 of 1950 as amended, you are hereby notified that I have this day included your name in the list on the grounds that you have been a member, office-bearer and active supporter of the said organization.[6]

Despite the party's banning, Josie remained politically active, speaking at public meetings of the Free Speech Convention, the Transvaal Peace Council, and the ANC.[7] After the CPSA was dissolved, its black members became active participants in the ANC. Josie again took up the issue of pass laws, but this time her focus was on the government threat to force African women to carry passes—something African women had successfully fought against decades previously.[8] Black women saw the reintroduction of passes as undermining their fragile hold on their existence in urban areas and as an assault on the integrity of their homes and family life. How would they stay with their husbands and look after their children if they were under constant threat of being expelled from their homes and sent to the Bantustans, the rural areas designated for black people that amounted to around 13 percent of the land? Maggie Resha summed up the reasons why black women so vigorously opposed pass laws:

> Women were fighting against the Pass Laws because of instinctive and self-protection from insecurity, degradation and humiliation. . . . And, from what they had experienced as mothers, wives and sweethearts of [male] passbearers, they were fighting to protect their families from being plunged into disarray. Last, but not least, they were fighting to protect their children from being turned into the street—wandering, hungry orphans when both parents were picked up and locked in jail or sold to white farmers for slave labour.[9]

On May 1, 1950, Josie chaired a multiracial conference of women that adopted a resolution to fight against pass laws for black women.[10] At an ANC meeting in Orlando Township on February 24, 1952, the Security Branch monitored her remarks:

> [Prime Minister] Malan has passed laws against the Non-Europeans. That bill includes a very important item, women are included to carry passes. This is Africa meant for the Africans. This is our country. Now they say that it is the white man's country, that will never happen. Then you will see the dead bodies of the Africans.[11]

She addressed another ANC meeting on April 27, 1952: "She gave the assurance that the women were determined to fight any oppressive measures that were introduced."[12]

Josie was referring to the Natives Abolition of Passes and Coordination of Documents Act, which Parliament was then considering. The act required all Africans born in the Union of South Africa aged sixteen and over to carry a standardized reference or passbook authorizing them to reside in a specified area. In particular, it required African women, who had not needed to carry passes for many decades, to do so. In addition, the Native Laws Amendment Act, passed the same year, mandated that every African, whether adult or child, had to receive a special permit to stay in an urban area for more than seventy-two hours.

Because women were already protesting against the law, the minister of native affairs, Hendrik Verwoerd, stated in Parliament that it was not the government's "intention to proceed with its practical application at the moment because we do not think the time is ripe for it."[13] Josie and other activists did not accept Verwoerd's word at face value. Anticipating that it was only a matter of time before the government applied passes to African women, they continued to speak out.

During the 1950s, women activists began placing the emphasis on "motherhood issues," such as protecting the integrity of the family, which allowed them to transcend class and racial differences.[14] That spirit contributed to the founding of FEDSAW, which was open to women of all races. Josie was a signatory to a letter inviting delegates to a conference on April 17, 1954, in Johannesburg to establish a national women's organization. At this meeting, the assembled 150 women adopted a charter calling for "equal rights for women regardless of race." The preamble stated:

> We, the women of South Africa, wives and mothers, working women and housewives, Africans, Indians, European and coloured, hereby declare our aim of striving for the removal of all laws, regulations, conventions and custom that discriminate against us as women, and that deprive us in any way of our inherent right to the advantages, responsibilities and opportunities that society offers to any one section of the population.

The charter prioritized working with men to challenge apartheid: "We women do not form a society separate from men. There is only one society and it is made up of both women and men. As women we share the problems and anxieties of our men, and join hands with them to remove social evils and obstacles to progress."[15] At the same time, it admonished men to support the advancement of women's rights: "We shall teach men they cannot hope to liberate themselves from the evils of discrimination and prejudice as long as they fail to extend to women complete and unqualified equality in law and in practice."[16] For Josie, this was reverting to her view in the 1930s that women should collaborate with men to challenge an unjust system but with the clear understanding that women were not prepared to work with men unless they addressed gender inequities.

When Josie's name was proposed for a leadership position in FEDSAW's national organization, some of its leaders had to be convinced of her commitment because she had become less involved in politics and more in the church. Ray Alexander, who had worked intimately with Josie in the party for several decades, was confident that she was still loyal to the cause and urged that she should be given a prominent post.[17] On July 4, 1954, she was elected president of FEDSAW's Transvaal branch and frequently spoke at its meetings. However, family responsibilities forced her to miss several meetings, and health ailments sapped her energy.[18] She suffered from osteoporosis and asthma, which she blamed on houses in Mzimhlophe being constructed of sand extracted from gold mine dumps.[19]

As a FEDSAW leader, she was involved in the discussions leading up to the Congress of the People in mid-1955, at which the Congress Alliance's Freedom Charter was adopted.[20] At a meeting on May 14, 1955, in Johannesburg, she said, "We have met here as mothers and citizens to proclaim our demands for the Freedom Charter of the people at the Congress of the People, Kliptown." On birth control, she added, "It is easy for the Whites to escape pregnancy, but we African women must have children regularly."

On May 29, at the Trades Hall in Johannesburg, Josie chaired a FEDSAW Transvaal meeting of two hundred

Figure 5.2. Josie Mpama/Palmer speaking at a meeting of the Federation of South African Women, 1954. (© Bailey's African History Archives; photo by Bob Gosani)

women who were discussing a pamphlet, *What Women Demand*, which was to be presented "to the convenors of the congress for incorporation into the Freedom Charter." At the meeting the women found common ground on "issues relating to health care, education, housing, social services and food." They also agreed on advocating the full equality of men and women in "political, legal, economic and marital" life.[21]

On several issues, however, there were heated discussions. For instance, on birth control, some argued that it was necessary to introduce family planning, while others contended that it would upset husbands who desired children. Helen Joseph, the FEDSAW Transvaal secretary, said some of those who opposed birth control were suspicious that it was a white ploy to reduce the black birth rate and increase the proportion of whites. Aware of how passionate both sides were on this issue, Josie could not find common ground for compromise.[22] She said, "Those who accept it, OK! Those who feel it is against their conscience, very well."[23]

This was a prelude to the Congress of the People held on June 25 and 26 at Kliptown in Soweto. Of the almost three thousand delegates, about a fourth were women—and Helen Joseph was the only woman who made a presentation, "What Women Demand."[24] The Freedom Charter, the congress's main product, did not highlight women's issues.[25]

In August, FEDSAW Transvaal followed up the adoption of the Congress Alliance's Freedom Charter with a gathering to promote the document. This came amid housing evictions in Sophiatown and police raids. Soon afterward, the newly established Black Sash, an organization of white women concerned about the government's attempts to remove Coloureds from the common voters' roll, began planning a march on the Union Buildings in Pretoria in October. FEDSAW, in co-operation with members of the ANC and its allies, lent its support.

In response, the government tried to disrupt the opposition by prohibiting large gatherings as well as banning scores of leaders of the Congress Alliance. On September 23, the minister of justice, Charles Swart, recognizing Josie's leadership in the protests, issued a five-year banning order prohibiting her "from attending . . . any gathering in any place within the Union of South Africa or the territory of South-West Africa." It was specifically timed to prohibit her from taking part in the planned protest action in Pretoria on October 27.[26]

The National Party invariably framed all its oppressive acts, such as banning orders, with legal precision. Hence, paragraph c of subsection 1 of section 5 of the Suppression of Communism Act of 1950 provided for banning orders to be served on opponents of the government. The law's determination of who was a communist was based on a set of definitions. Clause a of the definitions section stated that a communist was someone who advocated the doctrine of "Marxian socialism" espoused by Lenin, Trotsky, and the Comintern, but clause d was more expansive. It stated that a communist was anyone who "aims at the encouragement of feelings of hostility between the European and non-European races of the Union" that could advance communism.[27] The government wielded this clause to categorize their opponents as promoting hostility and thus define them as communists. As the Anglican priest Trevor Huddleston put it, "If they are Africans who show any powers of leadership . . . restriction is justified by the single word 'Communist.'"[28] The banning order empowered the government to silence leading dissidents without having to bring a formal charge against them in a court of law.

NOTICE IN TERMS OF PARAGRAPH (e) OF
SUBSECTION ONE OF SECTION FIVE OF THE
SUPPRESSION OF COMMUNISM ACT, 1950 (ACT
NO. 44 OF 1950), AS AMENDED.

WHEREAS your name appears on the list in the
custody of the officer referred to in section eight of the
abovementioned Act;

NOW THEREFORE, I, CHARLES ROBBERTS SWART, in
my capacity as Minister of Justice for the Union of South
Africa, by virtue of the powers conferred upon me by
paragraph (e) of subsection one of section five of the
Suppression of Communism Act, 1950 (Act No. 44 of 1950),
as amended, do hereby prohibit you from attending, during
a period of five years as from the date that this notice
is delivered or tendered to you, any gathering in any
place within the Union of South Africa or the territory
of South-West Africa.

Given under my hand at *Pretoria* on this
the *23rd* day of *September* 1955.

MINISTER OF JUSTICE.

TO: Josephine M'Pama,
10677(B) White City,
Orlando,
JOHANNESBURG.

Figure 5.3. South African government banning order of Josephine Mpama, September 23, 1955. (Josie Mpama/Palmer's
banning file)

Josie's banning order stipulated that she had to re-
sign any offices or discontinue her membership in a list
of forty-eight organizations, such as the ANC, the Save
our Children Committee, the South African Congress of

Trade Unions, the South African Society for Peace and Friendship with the Soviet Union, and the Transvaal Peace Council.

The day before the women's protest at the Union Building's amphitheater in Pretoria attracted several thousand demonstrators, Josie wrote her fellow activists in FEDSAW a fiery letter confirming that she had to withdraw from participating in the protest but expressing her continued belief in the triumph of the freedom struggle:

> My health has been a great barrier and has deprived me of my activities, but when one is told to shut-up in the face of bitter times ahead; when our women are going to be forced to carry passes, our children pushed back from the spark of light that they were enjoying to the dark days of Africa when they will become only be able to serve their masters, all those laws and legislations that bind us and force us to hold our tongues shall come to an end one day. Never were the minds of human beings controlled. Never were the eyes of human beings closed to what is happening unless that person goes blind. It is therefore natural that every living soul will ultimately see and follow the road to FREEDOM.
>
> Josie or no Josie the struggle will go on and ours will be the day of victory.[29]

The government's announcement that African women would be issued passbooks beginning in January 1956 triggered numerous demonstrations and pass burnings around the country. FEDSAW, whose new president was Lillian Ngoyi, an Orlando resident, started planning another march on Pretoria, for August 9.[30] This time an estimated twenty thousand women converged on the amphitheater at the Union Building to present written protests against the pass laws to Prime Minister Hans Strijdom, who was conspicuously absent.

Another policy that galvanized opposition was the Bantu Education Act of 1953, which consigned most Africans students to inferior educations. The minister of native affairs, Hendrik Verwoerd, was unashamedly blunt about the measure's intent: "Natives will be taught from childhood to realize that equality with the Europeans is not for them."[31] The Bantu Education Act took black education out of missions' hands and placed it directly under the control of the government.

Josie did not want her grandchildren scarred by the act. She had limited resources to send them to church-sponsored schools, so she turned to her Anglican network and successfully appealed to some Anglican priests to arrange a bursary from the Ekuthuleni Fund for her granddaughter Belinda in 1958 to attend an Anglican school in Swaziland where the wives of the communists Dan Tloome and J. B. Marks also taught.[32] She placed another granddaughter Lorraine at a Catholic school in Soweto.[33] She encouraged her granddaughters to keep in touch with current events by reading newspapers. According to Belinda, one of her favorite sayings was "There's no such thing as an old newspaper. If you haven't read the news, the news never gets stale." Another was "If you don't work, you don't eat."

After the Sharpeville Massacre on March 21, 1960, the South African government declared a state of emergency and rounded up opposition figures in a wide swoop regardless of whether they were still active in politics.[34] Josie was detained the day after the massacre and taken to the women's prison at the Fort, the Johannesburg prison that is now on the grounds of democratic South Africa's Constitutional Court. The Fort was a prison for both white and black detainees, including black women who had been arrested for illegal beer brewing and for protesting in 1958 against the pass laws.[35] It had a reputation for its abusive warders and unsanitary cells.

Because restrictions were placed on who could visit detainees, only Josie's daughter Hilda, who then worked for the Johannesburg City Council, was permitted to see her. Black and white detainees were segregated in prison facilities, but they still managed ways of communicating with each other by sending notes through "ordinary" prisoners who were there on criminal charges. Josie was eventually moved to Pretoria Central Prison (without Hilda being told) and let out after a few weeks. Josie complained afterward that the detention adversely affected her health.

In subsequent years, Special Branch police would regularly visit her to see if she was involved in political activities and to search for prohibited materials. A neighborhood policeman alerted her that it was his responsibility to keep an eye on her, so she was very careful about where she placed sensitive materials. Virginia Palmer related that a friend returning from the United States brought Josie a recording of Martin Luther King's "I Have a Dream" speech. After her family listened to it, she hid it away so well that they did not find it again until after she passed away.

6

Comrades and Christians

In the 1940s, Josie made several decisions that shaped the rest of her life. First, she joined the Anglican Church and devoted her energy to church women's groups. She did not see her embrace of Christianity and communism as contradictory but rather as expressions of her commitment to social justice. Second, Josie moved from Sophiatown to Mzimhlophe, a newly opened township in an area southwest of Johannesburg that came to be known as Soweto.[1] Largely through her involvement in church women's associations, she became an important figure in the township, providing a watchful presence in her neighborhood and treating people with ailments based on her knowledge of Afrikaner folk medicine. In the later years of her life, she lent her support to her grandchildren, who were active in the Soweto uprising of 1976.

In the late 1940s, Josie began participating actively in the Anglican Church. Her family had been long-time Methodists, but when her son Dennis began attending Christ the King Anglican Church in Sophiatown, he was so enthusiastic about it that Josie and some of her children also joined. Her decision was not a result of

Figure 6.1. Josie Mpama/Palmer in church uniform with children. (Palmer family album)

disillusionment with the CPSA but a recognition that the church was critical for serving her family, spiritual, and community needs at that time in her life.

One can speculate about the reasons why. A major factor was her family. She had committed several decades to political activism, often at the cost of spending time with her children. By the late 1940s, her daughters were adults and starting their own families. Hilda and Francis were both married at Christ the King. When they started having children of their own, they had to hold down jobs, and that meant that they turned to Josie to look after their kids. She raised five of her grandchildren in her home—and her rule with all of them was that when they entered her yard, they spoke Afrikaans.[2]

Her decision to join the Anglican Church was not surprising because Sophiatown had been the home of Father Trevor Huddleston, who arrived from England in 1943. He was appointed rector at Christ the King, and his brand of ecclesiastical activism and campaigning for social justice won him many supporters in the black community. The social gospel was a bridge between Christianity and communism because it preached that "the teachings of Christ constituted a revolutionary text for social change, a blueprint for transforming earth into heaven."[3] In other words, Christians should be actively involved in the world through caring for the poor and siding with the dispossessed. Some see this theology as compatible with socialist ideals. As Cheryl Carolus put it, "Socialism is the logical outworking of the New Testament ethic."[4] Or, as Chris Hani saw it, "In some ways, Marxism is a secular expression of a biblical social vision."[5]

Josie was not the only Communist Party member who found a home in Anglican women's organizations. The anthropologist Mia Brandel-Syrier interviewed a Mrs. X, a party member before it was banned, who told her that she still was a convinced communist and even inclined to supporting violence to overturn apartheid. "I am too extreme," she informed Brandel-Syrier. "Once you are a politician you can't be religious." Yet she was an active member of the women's guild known as a *Manyano* (unity) in her church. "But that is not a Manyano," she explained. "It is more advanced, more practical; we have speakers and lecturers and no praying and preaching. We come together once a month, and do sewing. We sew the church-clothes and priest-garments, so beautiful, and we do sick-visiting."[6] She added that she could not imagine a European communist sewing "priest-garments, so beautiful."

For many African communists, there was no contradiction between being a communist and a Christian. In his autobiography, Nelson Mandela referred to comrades who were communists and yet remained stalwarts in their church. On a visit to Cape Town, he met with Johnson Ngwevela and Greenwood Ngotyana, activists in the ANC and communists who were staunch Wesleyan Methodists. They worked on political issues every day of the week except for the Sabbath, which they set aside for the church. Mandela observed, "Communism and Christianity, at least in Africa, were not mutually exclusive."[7]

That was the case for Chris Hani when he joined an underground cell of the Communist Party in 1960. He noted, "I was still very much a Christian, attending church and participating in the various programmes of the Church. The Party and the Church were for me complementary institutions. I saw positively no contradiction between them."[8]

A comparative example from America of rank-and-file African American communists in Alabama who remained members of both a church and the party reinforces this point. Robin Kelley's magnificent study *Hammer and Hoe* recounts that in Montgomery, Alabama, the black working class understood exploitation and the class struggle through their grounding in prophetic Christianity, and it became a way through which people were drawn into the party. The party would open its meetings with prayer, and "Party literature produced locally [in Alabama] virtually never attacked religion."[9]

A related element to this subject is how noncommunist blacks in South Africa viewed the CPSA. The Suppression of Communism Act defined a communist as anyone who challenged the apartheid system, thus allowing the state to ban and arrest many activists who were not members of the party and prosecute them as if they were. Hence, many black people did not define the party by its ideology but as an organization fighting for their freedom. Albertina Sisulu, an ANC member who never joined the party, said that the CPSA's successor, the South African Communist Party (SACP) was "the first to fight against social and economic injustice in this country and therefore I instinctively support the Party."[10]

We have no evidence that Josie joined the underground Communist Party and the newly formed SACP when it was established in 1953, but we do know that she did not deny her past membership in the CPSA. Her granddaughters related that, to her, the Communist Party could do no wrong and that she always referred to the Soviet Union in glowing terms. She called on her granddaughters to deliver copies of the radical newspaper *New Age* to subscribers in her area. And FEDSAW leader Helen Joseph and well-known communists such as Dan Tloome, Moses Kotane, and Yusuf Dadoo still frequented her home.[11]

Mzimhlophe

Before the National Party came to power, the South African government had for years tried to clear black slum yards and to move black people as far away from white areas as possible. In Johannesburg, municipal officials started creating black townships at Diepkloof and Klipspruit, two farms about nine miles southwest of the city.[12] Orlando Township was the first to be established in 1931. However, during World War II, there was a dramatic increase in the movement of Africans, especially women, from rural areas into Johannesburg; by the end of the war, Johannesburg's black population had risen by over a half million. There was no accommodation for many of these new arrivals, and in places like Orlando people without housing began invading patches of open land and establishing squatter camps. The massive housing shortage led the government to establish new townships adjacent to Orlando to accommodate them. In 1947, it opened up Mzimhlophe next to Orlando. That was where Josie moved several years later and where she resided the rest of her life.

Josie secured accommodation through the assistance of one of her foster sons, Samuel, a YMCA employee, who had been allocated a house—number 10677—in Mzimhlophe. Because it was extremely difficult for a single woman to qualify for a township house, she was fortunate when Samuel allowed her to live in it. After the Group Areas Act was passed in 1950 segregating residential areas, Johannesburg municipal officials tried to remove her from Mzimhlophe to Noordgesig, a Coloured township near Orlando, by exchanging her house in Mzimhlophe for one there, but Josie successfully fought the order. That was a telling decision because Josie, with her racially mixed background, could have chosen to be classified as Coloured and live in a Coloured township, as did several of her stepsisters.[13]

People were arbitrarily thrown together in townships like Mzimhlophe, so it was critical for residents like Josie to establish community organizations and moral boundaries in neighborhoods. In 1949, she and a group of women started the Service Committee, which later developed into the African Self-Help Association. She recalled, "We also started a crèche . . . as it was very worrying to see so many small children roaming aimlessly about while their mothers were at work."[14] She participated in the Association of African and European

Women, which concentrated on working women who had to leave their children at home unattended.

Josie also devoted her energy to church activities. When Josie moved to Mzimhlophe, Anglicans met in an Anglican school building until St. Augustine's Church, staffed by priests of the Church of the Resurrection, Trevor Huddleston's order, was opened in 1954.

At St. Augustine's, she was an active member of the Church Women's Society (CWS), whose main objective was to raise money for the church. She was one of the leaders in raising money for the new church in Mzimhlophe by sewing clothes and selling these items at bazaars. Her special responsibility was washing the linen for the altar.

She also participated in the Ekuthuleni Church Committee and CWS. Both these groups arranged school bursaries for needy children, washed the altar linen, sewed clothes, raised money for the church by making soup, and looked after the poor and the sick by putting together food parcels.

Josie's concern for the poor and the less fortunate was another point of intersection between her support for the CPSA and the church. Both were addressing practical issues and offering services to others—and her involvement in church women's groups dovetailed with her commitment to organizing women beginning in the 1940s. Josie was engaging in what Iris Berger and some other scholars call "public healing," activities in which women utilized "their powers to insure individual health and well-being, and to mend relations between individuals and their communities."[15]

Josie expected her grandchildren to attend church on a regular basis. Sometimes they chafed at her strict rules. Virginia related that one time she "frog-marched" them to church on a snowy day and that when they returned home, she refused to allow them to play outside because it was too cold.[16]

Josie had a generous heart. From the 1930s on, as we have already noted in Samuel's case, she took in street children and young adults under her wing and treated them as if they were part of her family. Her children remembered Selby, Penwell Mnguni, Johnny, and Fred "Nippy" Masole, who later became an Anglican priest.

Another was Maggie Nkwe, whose parents, a mine worker and a domestic worker, raised her as best they could in a shantytown in Soweto.[17] She only started school in 1948 at the age of ten, but she took her schooling very seriously and was able to advance herself. As a high school student, she decided to attend St. Augustine's, where Josie oversaw the Sunday school. Maggie and Josie's granddaughter Belinda were in the same age group, and the pair grew up like twins under Josie's supervision. One of their responsibilities was cleaning the church chapel and making sure everything was in order. Maggie put it this way: "It was like escaping from my other depressing life at home. I looked forward to going to chapel before going to school." After Sunday school, she would go to "Aunt Josie's" home, where she would serve tea on trays. Maggie wondered why she would treat her in such a wonderful manner. She credited Josie with converting her from being a victim of circumstance to becoming a victor in control of her own fate.

One of the Sunday school teachers was David Nkwe, who fell for Maggie. She ignored his letters at first but eventually warmed up to him and ultimately accepted his marriage proposal as he walked her from Josie's place. By then Maggie regarded Josie and her family as her own family, and she asked Josie's daughter, Francis, to accompany her to meet her fiancé's family. Josie organized the wedding reception for them on December 17, 1960, at St. Augustine's church hall and made Maggie feel like she was a "royal princess."

Maggie attributed her life of service to Josie. When people ask her why she works for the betterment of her community, she explains, "I was brought up that way, I was nurtured by Josie Mpama."

Josie also made her presence felt in her neighborhood, where she was known as "Auntie Josie."[18] Her neighbors described her as someone who was very humble, gave good advice, and "one person who would never sit and fold up her arms." She could be very blunt—she did not hesitate to tell people, especially children in the street, when they were going wrong. Her neighbors all agreed that in present times this was not something to which children responded positively—and they regretted that change.

161

One of the women remembered an occasion when Josie found her outside "dismantling" her husband. Josie upbraided her, telling her that this was not how you dealt with your husband. She did not care whether one was a man or a woman—she spoke her mind. A woman who lived on another block told a story about her daughter coming to visit her school friends on Josie's block. Josie stopped her one day and told her not to come back because her visits would only lead to trouble with the boys.

Josie also had a reputation in her neighborhood for her command of Afrikaner folk remedies utilizing home medicines, roots, and herbs (*kruie*), which she must have picked up as a girl in Potchefstroom.[19] People would consult her about what medicines to use for a variety of ailments. As a midwife, she relied on a medicine called Wonderkroom to induce labor. When a Mrs. Lichaba was about to give birth, a nurse told her to wait another day, but Josie recommended that she take Wonderkroom instead. Her granddaughter Virginia related that when she was having a problem with her womb, she consulted a doctor who recommended surgery. But Josie insisted that she could treat her with a home medicine and cured her.

Josie was well known in her community for organizing women and teaching them how to bake, sew, and plant vegetables. She formed a women's cooperative for buying items together to save money. For the men who collected trash, she prepared soup in the winter and served them tea in the summer.[20]

Figure 6.2. Josie Mpama/Palmer with a friend. (Hilda Johnson)

To earn extra money in the 1970s, Josie relied on washing coats for a physician in the city. The doctor required extra starch, which Josie provided. She also washed for the Shanty Clinic in Mzimhlophe.[21]

The Soweto Uprising of 1976

Although she was careful about overtly involving herself in politics after the CPSA was outlawed, she educated her grandchildren about the injustices of the apartheid system and how it exploited black workers and encouraged them to be active and fight for their rights. Her grandchildren took up her opposition to an education system that made it extremely difficult for black students to advance themselves. This came to a head in mid-1976 when Transvaal officials mandated that half of subjects taught in black schools had to be in

Afrikaans, a language of which few black teachers had command. On June 16, when Soweto students took to the streets to protest their inferior education, the government responded brutally, killing over five hundred and targeting many others for arrest.[22]

Three of Josie's grandchildren took part in the Soweto Uprising. One of the persons police were searching for was Lorraine, Hilda's daughter. Her awareness of the political activism of her grandparents, Josie and Edwin Mofutsanyana, laid the foundation for her own political consciousness. Twenty-eight at the time of the student protests and working as a secretary for the National Union of South African Students at Witwatersrand University, she was heavily involved in organizing protests. When the police became aware of her activities, they raided the family home with dogs in the deep of night, demanding that her younger sister, Bella, tell them where they believed Lorraine was hiding bombs. To protect Lorraine, Josie hid her in a coal bin at the side of her home.[23] Several years later, Lorraine left the country and joined Umkhonto we Sizwe, the ANC's armed wing, in Angola.

During the student protests, Josie called Maggie Nkwe to tell her about how bad things were in Mzimhlophe. The police, she reported, were attacking and arresting schoolchildren, and when the police vans would pass her house, she heard their screams. Nkwe knew Molly Slaar, the wife of Johannesburg's mayor, who participated in Women for Peace, a moderate multiracial group founded by Bridget Oppenheimer in the wake of the Soweto Uprising. After Nkwe informed Slaar what Josie had told her, she contacted other members of the group. They immediately called the Protea police station. The officer in charge got very angry about the report and said he was going to investigate. The next thing Nkwe knew, she was called in by the superintendent and matron at Baragwanath Hospital where she worked and asked who told her the information she had passed on to Women for Peace. Nkwe said it was "Auntie" Josie. Josie soon received a letter from the police telling her to report to the Protea station, but she refused to go. She told them that if they wanted her, they could come to her home. They never responded.

Josie died on December 3, 1979, of injuries she incurred in a freak accident a month before. She had been hit by a car while standing in a queue of elderly people waiting for their pensions at Uncle Tom's Hall in Soweto. The car had been parked on an incline, and when its parking brake somehow was released, it careened into the group.[24]

Her burial at Avalon Cemetery drew a small gathering. Because of an intimidating police presence, people were too scared to come, although some brave souls such as Helen Joseph attended, and ANC flags were defiantly displayed.

Several months after her death, a longtime friend, Walter Sisulu, then in his sixteenth year of imprisonment

Figure 6.3. Gravestone of Josie Mpama/Palmer at Avalon Cemetery with great-granddaughter Nicolai Allard standing next to it. This new marker was erected in 2018. (Photo by Sally Gaule)

on Robben Island, wrote Josie's daughter Carol to express his condolences to her family:

> In her last visit to the Island, my wife told me of the death of our friend, mother and a comrade, our beloved mother, Josie. She was certainly the tower of strength not only to your family but to many families and the African people in general, nay to the people of S.A. [South Africa]. I have had the pleasure and

honour of working with her and as such became associated with the whole family. It is, therefore, fit and proper that on such occasion I should pay my last respects.

Do kindly accept our condolences you and your entire family, your sister Hilda and all the members of Josie's family. It is always painful to remind bereaved families of the unhappy past events. I however, hope you will bear with me if appears to be opening up the healing wounds.

All is well in our end. We keep ourselves fit and healthy as far as possible. We are for ever looking forward to a day of re-union.[25]

Conclusion

Get Up and Get Moving

Although Josie Mpama/Palmer is best known for her political activism, she performed many roles throughout her lifetime: mother, grandmother, community and churchwomen organizer, and healer. She displayed courage and resilience in taking on and overcoming adversity at all stages of her life. In her youth, she battled to find stability in her family and home life. As an adult, she valiantly fought against racist laws and regulations that undermined the survival and sanctity of black families and communities. A domestic servant and laundress at various times in her life, she was especially mindful of the tenuous conditions that black women and their families endured and understood the bread-and-butter issues that could mobilize them.

Josie was indeed an "untidy hero" who troubled the waters and challenged racial, ethnic, gender, and class conventions and boundaries—set by segregation and apartheid or by communities themselves:

- As the daughter of an African man and a mixed-race woman, she transgressed rigid racial identification in her personal and political lives.

As an Afrikaans-speaking, mixed-race woman who identified as African and lived in Soweto for the last three decades of her life, she chose to defy apartheid conventions that attempted to divide people into arbitrary racial classifications.

- Josie promoted nonracialism. She chose to join political organizations that were open to people of different racial groups such as the CPSA and the NEUF, and she pioneered women's groups such as the Transvaal All Women's Union and the Federation of South African Women that were open to women of all races.

- She was a black internationalist in the 1930s, drawing inspiration from the Soviet Union and the Communist International for their support of oppressed peoples globally and freedom for black people in South Africa.

- She was one of the first black women to join the CPSA and remained with the party from its nadir in the 1930s through its revival in the 1940s. A party loyalist on some issues, she was often an independent voice who criticized the party on internal issues and racial friction within the party in the late 1930s.

- She bluntly challenged the patriarchal attitudes of African men who restricted African women to domestic roles and blocked them from participating in the public political arena. She raised questions about whether women should work cooperatively with men in political activities. Her views evolved from supporting the joint participation of women with men to advocating that women go it alone in their own organizations.

- Even as Josie remained a prominent person in the CPSA in the 1940s, she renewed her Christian beliefs and began actively participating in the Anglican Church. She did not see Christianity and communism on opposite ends of a spectrum. Rather, she found common ground in the commitments of the CPSA and the Anglican Church to social justice and serving the poor.

Starting with her childhood, Josie developed inner strength, self-reliance, and resilience, which she drew on throughout her life. In an interview that appeared in *Drum* magazine in 1975, she made some observations about her life of service that are a fitting epitaph for her life:

> I am not as young and fit as I once was, but I will continue to do whatever I can to uplift my people. We women are the backbone of the nation and I would like to see many more women take an active interest in developing the community. We need more crèches, more schools and recreation centres to curb juvenile

delinquency. We also need old-age homes. But we will not be given these things on a plate—we have to work for them. So I would like to end by saying to all my sisters—get up and get moving![1]

It is significant that Josie made her comments at a time when the apartheid regime was tightening its repressive controls over black people. Rather than retreating, she encouraged black people—and women in particular—to assume responsibility for their lives, to bounce back from adversity, and to be resourceful and take the initiative in developing their communities on their own. She stressed that they would not be handed anything on a platter—they had "to work for them"—and challenged her sisters to "get up and get moving."

Josie died as the apartheid system was entering its last phase. Her grandchildren's activism surely gave her a taste of what was coming, because a year after her interview, the Soweto Uprising erupted. In the early 1980s, internal resistance to the apartheid regime intensified, with trade unions, civic groups, and regional and national organizations challenging it. Under mounting pressure domestically and internationally, some National Party leaders finally realized that the time had come to reach a settlement with the opposition. After President F. W. de Klerk unbanned leading opposition parties such as the ANC, the South African Communist Party, and the Pan Africanist Congress in early 1990 and released political prisoners such as Nelson Mandela, many of the contending groups participated in difficult and protracted negotiations to work out a compromise solution. Finally, in April 1994, elections were held in which all South Africans were able to vote for the first time in the country's history. A government of national unity led by President Nelson Mandela came into office.

The 1994 democratic elections not only brought about the kind of political freedom that Josie had long fought for but also a different political landscape for women, as they moved from opposing the apartheid state to participating in the new democracy. A significant number of women took seats in Parliament and provincial assemblies. Ironically, the access women gained to state power contributed to a diminution of their participation in grassroot organizing. Although gender and sexual rights are now enshrined in the constitution, that has not generally significantly eroded patriarchal controls over authority and power. As we can see with the feminization of HIV/AIDS and the epidemic of violence and sexual assaults against women, Josie's admonition to women to get up and get moving remains relevant.

Josie Mpama/Palmer on Gender and Politics

Letter, "Educating our Bantu Women," *Mochochonono*, 22 November 1933.

Editor, Dear Sir,—

Kindly allow me space in your paper for the following which is a reply to an article which appeared in your paper headed as above.[1]

Dear Sir,—

In this same paper you gave your opinion as regards Education for Native women. I must say that I agree with you to a certain extent, in the first place I must say that as far as religion is concerned Native women are playing a very important part such as no other race plays. A woman may be how educated, how un-educated, or how backward but the fact remains that in all different Churches we have here today women are in the majority in membership. And here I don't agree with you when you say that our women should be given more Education on religious lines. To day with all the misery that women are faced with they can only tell you that the Europeans will only oppress us as long as God will allow them to do so, and God will pay them one day for all the wrong done to the Natives today. Which I personally think is very wrong that unless we as a nation entitled to live in freedom wake up and demand that freedom, we shall wait until doomsday for God to revenge.

It is quite true as you say that some people say women are inferior to men, but in most cases those men who are politically advanced are to be blamed for the backwardness of their wives, sisters and daughters. For instance most men will go out to either sports meetings etc etc, and never have the slightest thought of taking their womenfolk with them. All they are concerned with is to come back and find hot dinners awaiting them. Amongst all our leaders it is very seldom that one will see their wives or women friends accompanying them to meetings, and in all their struggles only few women take active part, except in locations when such struggles for lodgers permits are fought then some who cannot afford to pay such fees, and because it affects the family as a whole then they find that there is no other way out than to unite with the others and attend meetings. Then as soon as they find that they have either won or lost they go back home and take to their domestic spheres.

Sometimes one wonders what is really the cause of our non European women not taking part in any political organizations especially here in town where meetings of all organizations are daily carried on and we suffer most.

I agree that women have the same intellect as men and that is clearly demonstrated today by the Government who shows us that Native women are equal to men, by forcing them to carry night specials after 10 30 p.m. The constables on duty demand a special pass from a man next from his partner. Whereas there has long been a cry from the men that the government should release them from this burden of slavery, the Government's reply is that "I shall release you by forcing your wives to assist you to carry them." Is this not the time for women to wake up and to say my place is no longer in the kitchen but on the political platform to demand my rights?

In town we have such things as pick ups, in every meeting that is held by a working class movement. Resolutions are passed urging the Government to remove these criminal creators which even pick up women, but nowhere is our Native women to be seen. Is it because they are satisfied with this brutal treatment? No it is only that they are accustomed to the back seat where they have no say, and are told that womens [sic] places are in the kitchens. And I know that we have enough educated women who if only they are told what an important part they can play in the political field, will not hesitate to do so.

And as an African woman, I appeal to all class of conscious [sic] men and women to wake up their women folk in this struggle, and this can be done if only pains are taken to do so. Let our Mothers, Sisters and Daughters be educated politically and stand on the forefront with the leaders of all countries and demand freedom and equality for all than to remain being religious and allow themselves to be haunted by police every where they go. For it is only when Natives are politically advanced that they can and will have advanced education[ally], socially, economically and commercially.

"An Appeal to African Women Join the Struggle against Oppressive Laws," *South African Worker,* **January 30, 1937.**

A year has passed since the Native Bills were passed and to-day we are faced with a new bill to amend the laws relating to Natives in urban areas.

There are Natives who maintain that the reading of the bill could not take place without the consent of the Native Representative Council. There are others who do not believe that such a bill can be passed in this period of "prosperity and progress." That the Government is determined to get the bill through was shown by the first reading, which took place on Tuesday, the 12th Jan. This is the beginning of a hard struggle which confronts all African men and women. Very few women took part in the struggle against the Native Bills, probably because not having had the vote they did not think it important to assist their men to maintain the vote.

Now we have a bill that is going to drive Natives back to the land when the authorities find it necessary to do so, is going to regulate the recruiting and employment of Native labourers. We know that this bill is seriously taken up by the men and we wonder whether the women also see the dangers with which they are confronted. Fathers, brothers, husbands and sons have flocked into towns not only because living conditions and treatment were better, but mainly because wages are higher and here is the danger of BEING DRIVEN BACK TO THE LAND WITH THE FAMILIES and ALL.

We, women, should come on to the field as strugglers, for only with our help can our men fight successfully against this new bill. Only by joint struggle can we compel Grobler and Co. to withdraw this new slave law.

Women, we can no longer remain in the background or concern ourselves only with domestic and sports affairs. The time has arrived to enter the political field and stand shoulder to shoulder with their men in the struggle.

It was owing to the existence of the All African Convention that we have been offered half a loaf. Had we been truly united we would have won the battle.

Women of Africa, I appeal to you to loose [sic] no time, but come forward and take your place in the struggle against the oppressive laws inflicted on you.

Come to-day for to-morrow it will be too late.

"African Women Must Be Organised We Are Prepared to Move," *South African Worker,* June 26, 1937.

Working women, unemployed women, peasant women and house-wives! An open war of terror has been declared on your as well as on our menfolk. The past four weeks have been weeks of unrest in all locations. As early as four o'clock on Saturday and Sunday mornings you are disturbed from your sound-sleep by police raiding for passes, poll tax, beer etc. Why have we got this attack on the locations? Simply because the location Councils have decided to open beer canteens, which is disapproved of by the masses. Our conclusion is this, that the police have decided to terrify you to such an extent that instead of boycotting the canteens, which is the general feeling, you will be so scared that the canteens will be opened without the least resistance.

We will find that as far as our menfolk are concerned the present pass raids are to check up on the number of unemployed who are roaming about. We see that the Amendment to the Urban Areas Act is providing cheap labor for the farmers. This means that anybody who is not in the employ of a European will be forced to work for a farmer for whatever he wishes to pay.

Women Must Be Mobilised alongside Men

Now what are we as African women going to do? We must remember that no successful fight can be waged unless the broad masses of women are drawn into it. And agitation alone will not accomplish this. We must find a way of mobilizing the masses of women for the struggle against high rents, low wages, mass arrests and evictions, for better houses, free medical attendance, higher and better education, home brewing of beer for personal consumption and for social equality.

Can this be attained? By forming separate women['s] organisations according to the situation in each instance. For this the Council of African Women formed at Bloemfontein with the first Conference of the All-African Convention in 1935, would have served the purpose; unfortunately we see that this organisation fell into the hands of leaders who buried it; leaders who think that this Council covers the field and leaves no space for another organisation but do *not give a lead*. Therefore they must make way [for] women who will lead and make a move to carry out the work.

Happenings of the past have proved the necessity of having women's organisations spread all over the country. And for this it is necessary to seek out the simplest and most flexible forms, in order to establish contact and bring about co-operation in the struggle.

It is today or never! We do not expect to undergo worse than we have done in the past. No matter how effective a struggle our men put up it will prove fruitless without our help.

I appeal to all African women to stand by and face the common enemy—namely our oppressors.

Notes

Introduction: An Untidy Hero

1. "Comfort in Moscow for Josie," *Drum*, June 8, 1975.

2. The government awarded her stepsister, Vesta Smith, the Order of Luthuli in 2008.

3. Iris Berger, *Threads of Solidarity: Women in South African Industry* (Bloomington: Indiana University Press, 1992); Helen Scanlon, *Representation and Reality: Portraits of Women's Lives in the Western Cape, 1948–1972* (Cape Town: HSRC Press, 2007); Cherryl Walker, *Women and Resistance in South Africa* (New York: Monthly Review Press, 1991); Shireen Hassim, *Women's Organization and Democracy in South Africa* (Madison: University of Wisconsin Press, 2006); Julia Wells, *We Now Demand! The History of Women's Resistance to Pass Laws in South Africa* (Johannesburg: Witwatersrand University Press, 1993); and Nomboniso Gasa, ed., *Women in South African History: They Remove Boulders and Cross Rivers* (Cape Town: HSRC Press, 2007).

4. Emma Gilboy Keller, *Lady: The Life and Times of Winnie Mandela* (London: Vintage, 1994); Alan Wieder, *Ruth First and Joe Slovo in the War against Apartheid* (New York: Monthly Review Press, 2013); Zubeida Jaffer, *Beauty of the Heart: The Life and Times of Charlotte Manye Maxeke* (Bloemfontein: Sun Media, 2016); and Elinor Sisulu, *Walter and Albertina Sisulu: In Our Lifetime* (Cape Town: David Philip, 2002).

5. Helen Joseph, *Side by Side: The Autobiography of Helen Joseph* (New York: William Morrow, 1986); Ellen Kuzwayo,

Call Me Woman (Johannesburg: Ravan, 1995); Maggie Resha, *Mangoana Tsoara Thipa Ka Bohaleng: My Life in the Struggle* (Johannesburg: Congress of South African Writers, 1991); Ray Alexander, *All My Life and All My Strength* (Johannesburg: STE Publishers, 2004); and Emma Mashinini, *Strikes Have Followed Me All My Life: A South African Autobiography* (New York: Routledge, 1991).

6. Walker, *Women and Resistance,* 26. For instance, the major chapters by Tom Lodge and Saul Dubow on twentieth-century political change in *The Cambridge History of South Africa* do not mention women at all. See *The Cambridge History of South Africa,* vol. 2, ed. Robert Ross, Anne Mager, and Bill Nasson (Cambridge: Cambridge University Press, 2011).

7. *The Star,* November 19, 2012.

8. See Mia Roth, "Josie Mpama: The Contribution of a Largely Forgotten Figure in the South African Liberation Struggle," *Kleio* 28 (1996): 120–36. Roth focuses primarily on Mpama's views on the CPSA during the mid-1930s.

Chapter 1: Family Matters

1. LD 1228 AG 791/06, National Archives of South Africa (NASA), Pretoria.

2. Nelson Mandela, *Long Walk to Freedom* (Randburg: Macdonald Purnell, 1994), 38–39.

3. Mandela, 43.

4. Solomon Plaatje, "The Essential Interpreter," in *Sol Plaatje: Selected Writings,* ed. Brian Willan (Athens: Ohio University Press, 1997), 53. I thank Brian Willan for this reference. On Plaatje, see Willan's magnificent biography, *Sol Plaatje: A Life of Solomon Tshekiso Plaatje, 1876–1932* (Charlottesville: University of Virginia Press, 2019). For a discussion of black intermediaries such as interpreters and clerks during the colonial period, see the introduction to *Intermediaries, Interpreters, and Clerks: African Employees in the Making of Colonial Africa,* ed. Benjamin N. Lawrance, Emily Lynn Osborn, and Richard L. Roberts (Madison: University of Wisconsin Press, 2006), 3–37.

5. Andre Odendaal, *The Founders: The Origins of the African National Congress and the Struggle for Democracy in South Africa* (Lexington: University Press of Kentucky, 2013), 326–28.

6. Odendaal, 390–97. See also Martin Plaut, *Promise and Despair: The First Struggle for a Non-racial South Africa* (Athens: Ohio University Press, 2017).

7. The South African Native National Congress changed its name to the African National Congress in 1923. *Tsala ea Becoana,* August 26 and September 1, 1911. I thank Peter Limb for these references.

8. Divorce Case of Stephen Mpama and Georgina Mpama, Circuit Court of Potchefstroom, May 1910, TQB ZTPD 5/676 85/1910, Transvaal Archives, NASA, Pretoria.

9. "Autobiography of J. Mpama [1936]," in *South Africa and the Communist International: A Documentary History,* vol. 2, ed. Apollon Davidson, Irina Filatova, Valentin Gorodnov, and Sheridan Johns (London: Frank Cass, 2003), 160–70. Party members who attended Comintern schools in the Soviet Union were expected to write autobiographical essays before they returned home. As she was leaving to return to South Africa in 1936, Josie left hers on a nightstand in her hotel room. Comintern records are housed in the Rossiiskii gosurdarstvennyi arkhiv sotsial'no-politicheskoi istorii (Russian State Archive of Socio-Political History [RGASPI]); Josie's essay was filed in RGASPI 495.279.65. In this study, I have cited Comintern records with three sets of numbers. The first refers to the record group, the second to the category, and the third to the box number.

10. A "location" was a living area for black people segregated from a white town. The term "location" changed to "township" during the apartheid years after 1948.

11. Mpama, "Autobiography," 161.

12. A *sjambok* is a heavy leather whip three to five feet long, fashioned from the hide of a hippopotamus or a rhinoceros.

13. Mpama, "Autobiography," 164.

14. Mpama.

15. Mpama, 165.

16. "Bushmen" (a preferable name is San) were the earliest inhabitants of southern Africa and subsisted by hunting small

game and gathering wild plants and herbs. In the nineteenth century some white and black South Africans began using "Bushman" as a pejorative term to mean someone who was not civilized or was marginal to society. Even though Josie's mother's family was descended from a mixture of races and ethnicities, Stephen Mpama's relatives used "bushmans" as a slur.

17. Mpama, "Autobiography," 169.

18. This information about the biological fathers of Josie's children came from Carol and Francis, who knew nothing more about the men.

19. "Comfort in Moscow for Josie," *Drum,* June 8, 1975.

20. Magistrate, Potchefstroom to Secretary for Justice, Pretoria, January 23, 1913, Department of Justice (JD) 161 3/87/13, part 1, NASA.

21. Magistrate, Potchefstroom.

22. Whitehouse to Secretary of Justice, October 24, 1916, JD 161 3/87/13, part 1.

23. Stephen was engaged to Evelyn Skota of Kimberley in 1911, but apparently the marriage did not take place. *Tsala ea Batho,* October 7, 1911.

24. In South Africa, this is a Standard II education.

25. They had a third brother, Chalmers, who worked in the Native Affairs Department in Fordsburg. (Interview by Robert Edgar of Esme Matshikiza, Cape Town, February 16, 1995, and Vesta Smith, Noordgesig, March 6, 1995). Both Josiah and Stephen were property owners in Johannesburg. Josiah owned two plots of land in Sophiatown, which he bought in 1911 and 1912. Stephen owned two lots in Newclare worth about two hundred pounds. When Stephen's estate was divided after his death, his will stipulated that Josie should receive a tenth of his estate, as a payout estimated to be worth nineteen pounds, and that the rest should to go to his widow, Clara Emma. KJB 349 13/221, NASA.

26. The other three daughters were Vesta Valerie (April 15, 1917), Fairy Adelaide (February 4 1925), and Sheila Esme (September 1, 1927).

27. Her daughters remembered that their mother was horrified if they answered the phone in Afrikaans.

28. His successor in 1920 as chair of the mine clerks' association was A. W. G. Champion. *Umteteli wa Bantu,* August 7, 1920.

29. Death notice, SAB KJB 13/221, NASA.

30. *Umteteli wa Bantu,* May 14, 1927. Mpama was buried in grave 11470 in the C. K. (Cape Kaffir) section of the Braamfontein Cemetery. T. D. Mweli Skota included a sketch of Mpama's life in his *African Yearly Register, Being an Illustrated National Biographical Dictionary (Who's Who) of Black Folks in Africa* (Johannesburg: Esson (printer) 1931), 71.

In gold mines, compound indunas were blacks who worked with white compound managers and black mine police to maintain security.

Chapter 2: A Fighting Location

1. *Indian Opinion,* May 19, 1906. The location was called the "Place of Sod" because homes were constructed out of bricks of mud sod. Makweteng residents were allocated "stands" or pieces of land varying in size for which they paid rent,

2. Fanie Jansen van Rensburg, "Protest by Potchefstroom Native Location's Residents against Dominance, 1904 to 1950," *Historia* 57, no. 1 (2012): 23–41.

3. *Indian Opinion,* May 19, 1906.

4. Van Rensburg, "Protest," 25.

5. Julia Wells, "'The Day the Town Stood Still': Women in Resistance in Potchefstroom, 1912–1930," in *Town and Countryside in the Transvaal: Capitalist Penetration and Popular Response,* ed. Belinda Bozzoli (Johannesburg: Ravan, 1983), 274.

6. Wells, 275.

7. *Transvaal Leader,* March 18 and March 25, 1912, and *Indian Opinion,* April 6, 1912. Sharman was certainly a thorn in the town council's side. The town clerk wrote the Anglican bishop of Pretoria to complain that Sharman was dealing with people's material interests in a manner not becoming an "ordained minister of Christ's Church" and to threaten that he might not officially recognize Sharman as a representative of his church. The bishop defended Sharman by stating that his

concern for his congregants' spiritual and material needs was the "duty of every ordained Minister of Christ's Church." The bishop also rejected the town clerk's threat not to recognize Sharman as the Anglican priest of Potchefstroom. Town Clerk, Potchefstroom to Anglican Bishop of Pretoria, May 14, 1914, and Bishop of Pretoria to Town Clerk, March 7, 1914, Municipality of Potchefstroom (MPO), 2/1/1 22, NASA.

8. Wells, "'Day the Town Stood Still,'" 275.

9. Wells, 280.

10. Wells, 280; MPO 2/1/1 22.

11. Wells, "'Day the Town Stood Still,'" 281.

12. *Potchefstroom Herald,* September 11, 1925.

13. Paul Maylam, "The Rise and Decline of Urban Apartheid in South Africa," *African Affairs* 89, no. 354 (1990): 66–67.

14. Hoff, Superintendent of Location to Health and Parks Committee, Potchefstroom, January 1, 1923, MPO 2/1/356 959.

15. MPO 2/1/256 959. According to a *Potchefstroom Herald* news story of July 21, 1925, very few African women—about ten annually—were prosecuted.

16. *Potchefstroom Herald,* September 30, 1927.

17. *African Leader,* February 4, 1933.

18. MPO 2/1/60/2902.

19. *African Leader,* February 4, 1933.

20. Weeks to Town Clerk, Potchefstroom, January 5, 1928, MPO 2/1/105 1549. After attending the Congress of Location Superintendents in Johannesburg in November 1927, Weeks came away armed with information to support his view that residents in locations could be squeezed even further financially. He learned that the municipalities of Pietermaritzburg and Durban were making a profit from producing "kaffir beer," a home brew, whereas in Bloemfontein, where the municipality allowed residents to brew beer, it had been a failure. He called for the "municipalisation of Kaffir Beer" in Potchefstroom. In 1929, the town council passed a resolution placing the brewing of beer under the exclusive control of the municipal council and prohibiting brewing in location homes. Only one council member, Aletta Nel, noting that prohibitions on beer brewing had led to troubles in other cities such

as Durban, voted against the resolution. She was concerned that the municipality should not make a profit off Africans.

21. Petition of Registered Holders of Stands in the Location, May 30, 1928, to Mayor and Town Councillors of Potchefstroom, and Weeks to Town Clerk and Weeks to Town Clerk, Potchefstroom, January 2, 1928, MPO 2/1105 1549.

22. Benjamin Mohlomi to Mayor, Potchefstroom, October 28, 1929, MPO 2/1/105 1549.

23. *South African Worker,* February 28, 1929.

24. MPO 2/1/1 24.

25. *Sunday Times,* August 26, 1926.

26. *South African Worker,* March 30, 1928.

27. *South African Worker,* March 30, 1928.

28. *South African Worker,* May 11, 1928; Minutes, CPSA Executive, April 19, 1928, RGSAPI 495.64.75.

29. For more details on Mofutsanyana's life, see Robert Edgar, *The Making of an African Communist: Edwin Thabo Mofutsanyana and the Communist Party of South Arica, 1927–1939* (Pretoria: University of South Africa Press, 2005).

30. *Potchefstroom Herald,* November 23, 1928.

31. *Potchefstroom Herald,* December 6, 1929.

32. *Potchefstroom Herald,* August 9, 1930.

33. Dingaan's Day commemorated the defeat of a Zulu army by an Afrikaner force on December 16, 1838. To Afrikaner nationalists, it was celebrated as the Day of the Covenant and symbolized their divine destiny to be in Africa. To black opponents of the Union government, it began to be celebrated in the 1920s to remember and celebrate African resistance to white rule.

34. Julia Wells, *We Now Demand! The History of Women's Resistance to Pass Laws in South Africa* (Johannesburg: Witwatersrand University Press, 1993), 73.

35. Robert Edgar, interview with Edwin Mofutsanyana, July 1980, Roma, Lesotho; *South African Worker,* December 31, 1929; Bannister, Office of the District Commandant, Potchefstroom to Deputy Commissioner, South African Police, Pretoria, December 23, 1929, JD 547 9490/29.

36. *Potchefstroom Herald,* December 17 and 27, 1929.

37. JD 547 9490/29.

38. JD 547 9490/29.

39. Jack and Ray Simons, *Class and Colour in South Africa, 1850–1950* (London: Penguin, 1969), 423.

40. Although the town council generally sided with Weeks, it was not oblivious to the hardships the regulation imposed. It raised the age for lodger's permits to twenty-one, and it occasionally was prepared to give extensions when standholders were not able to pay or wrote off the arrears that had accumulated.

41. Wells, *We Now Demand!*, 72.

42. In 1866, the Methodist Church had had an inauspicious beginning in Potchefstroom for its African members when David Magatha, a Methodist evangelist, began preaching in the market square. Local whites, thinking that a black man preaching in public was "sacrilegious," seized him. He was "arrested, tied to the wheel of an ox-wagon, and publicly whipped, and . . . banished from Potchefstroom." He later arranged for a permit from President Marthinus Wessell Pretorius to resume preaching.

43. Five-page typed memo by Henderson on Potchefstroom struggle, RGASPI 495.14.348. Henderson was Josie's alias in Moscow.

44. Wells, *We Now Demand!*, 75.

45. Wells, 75.

46. Josephine Mpama to Secretary of Native Affairs, n.d., MPO 2/1/356/956.

47. John Allison to Josephine Mpama, March 7, 1930, MPO 2/1/356/956.

48. Town Clerk to Location Superintendent, January 16, 1930, MPO 2/1/356 956.

49. Weeks to Town Clerk, Potchefstroom, April 28, 1930, MPO 2/1/356 956.

50. Weeks to Town Clerk, March 13, 1931, MPO 2/1/356 956.

51. Town Clerk to Superintendent, September 15, 1931, MPO 2/1/356 956.

52. "Good boys" were blacks who were prepared to work in white-controlled institutions.

53. Five-page typed memo by Henderson.

54. Eugene Dennis to Comintern, September 16, 1932, and Report of Secretariat, CPSA, April 13, 1932, RGASPI 495.64.120.

55. Report of Secretariat, CPSA, April 13, 1932, RGASPI 495.64.120. Johannesburg had fifteen members, Evaton ten, Brakpan ten, Vereeniging ten, Pretoria five, and Cape Town eight.

56. Edgar, interview with Mofutsanyana.

57. Edgar, interview with Mofutsanyana.

58. Kotane, letter to comrades, July 31, 1934, RGASPI 495.64.133.

59. Wells, "Day the Town Stood Still," 286.

60. Interview, Julia Wells with Josie Mpama/Palmer, Mzimhlophe, October 1977.

61. Statement of Josie Palmer, RGASPI 495.64.141.

62. Sworn testimony of Joseph Sepeng, MPO 2/1/16 362.

63. Wells, "Day the Town Stood Still," 299.

Chapter 3: Party Battles

1. Martin Chanock, *The Making of South African Legal Culture, 1902–1936: Fear, Power and Prejudice* (Cambridge: Cambridge University Press, 2001), 147–49.

2. Chief Inspector, Witwatersrand Division, South African Police (SAP) to Commissioner, SAP, Pretoria, September 19, 1932, JD 1/333/30, part 4.

3. Witwatersrand Division, SAP, to Commissioner, SAP, October 6, 1932, JD 1/333/30, part 4.

4. Lt. Col., Deputy Commissioner, SAP, Witwatersrand Division, to Commissioner, SAP, November 15, 1932, JD 1/333/30, part 3,

5. Chief Inspector for Deputy Commissioner, Witwatersrand Division, SAP, Johannesburg to Commissioner, SAP, Pretoria, May 4, 1930, JD 1/333/30, part 4.

6. Allison Drew, *Between Empire and Revolution: A Life of Sidney Bunting, 1873–1936* (London: Pickering & Chatto, 2007), 151.

7. Allison Drew, *Discordant Comrades: Identities and Loyalties on the South African Left* (Burlington, VT: Ashgate, 2000), 94–126. Several CPSA members have published detailed ac-

counts of this factional fighting. See, e.g., Brian Bunting, *Moses Kotane: A South African Revolutionary; A Political Biography* (London: Inkululeko Publications, 1975), and Jack Simons and Ray Simons, *Class and Colour in South Africa, 1850–1950* (London: Penguin, 1969).

8. Drew, *Discordant Comrades,* 127.

9. RGASPI 495.64.141. The 64 refers to CPSA records.

10. The best discussion of KUTV's faculty and South African students is Irina Filatova and Apollon Davidson, *The Hidden Thread: Russia and South Africa in the Soviet Era* (Johannesburg: Jonathan Ball, 2013), 111–40.

11. While in Moscow, Mofutsanyana asked the Comintern International Contacts Section to send six pounds a month to support Josie and the children. The grant was approved and extended when Josie went to Moscow. Woodford McClellan, "Black Hajj to 'Red Mecca': Africans and Afro-Americans at KUTV, 1925–1938," in *Africa in Russia, Russia in Africa,* ed. Maxim Matusevich (Trenton, NJ: Africa World Press, 2007), 70.

12. McClellan, 111.

13. Woodford McClellan, "Africans and Black Americans in the Comintern Schools, 1925–1934," *International Journal of African Historical Studies* 26, no. 2 (1993): 371–90.

14. Mofutsanyana told me this in an informal conversation around 1985. Josie stated that Kotane was the father of one of her children on a biographical form she filled out in 1936 while attending KUTV. Mpama, "Autobiography of J. Mpama [1936]," in *South Africa and the Communist International: A Documentary History,* vol. 2, ed. Apollon Davidson, Irina Filatova, Valentin Gorodnov, and Sheridan Johns (London: Frank Cass, 2003), 160.

15. Hakim Adi, "The Communist International and Black Liberation in the Interwar Years," in *From Toussaint to Tupac: The Black International since the Age of Revolution,* ed. Michael West, William Martin, and Fanon Che Wilkins (Chapel Hill: University of North Carolina Press, 2009), 173.

16. Lt. Colonel, Deputy Commissioner, SAP, Witwatersrand Division, to Commissioner, SAP, November 15, 1932, JD 1/333/30, part 3.

17. "International Women's Day: The Struggle for the Emancipation of Women," *South African Worker,* March 18, 1937.

18. She was referring to Jane Batwa, a party member from Cradock.

19. Bunting, *Moses Kotane,* 39.

20. In her history of the CPSA, Mia Roth confuses Josie with another Palmer, Albertina Alexandra. This is likely because in one of Alexandra Palmer's files in the South African National Archives there is a document about Josie. Hence, Roth mistakenly asserts that Josie got to the Soviet Union on a path that took her to South West Africa and Angola. Claiming to be a daughter of the Zulu king Dinuzulu, Alexandra Palmer eventually made her way to France, where she married a Frenchman. After the French government refused to recognize her citizenship there, she tried to obtain British citizenship by virtue of her South African ancestry. In another place, Roth identifies Mabel Palmer as Josie based on a footnote in Peter Walshe's *The Rise of African Nationalism in South Africa,* 195. However, Walshe was referring to Mabel Palmer, a University of Natal academic. Mia Roth, *The Communist Party in South Africa: Racism, Eurocentricity and Moscow, 1921–1950* (Johannesburg: Partridge Africa, 2016), 187–90.

21. Julius's family had immigrated to South Africa from Latvia in 1907, while Matilda's had emigrated from Lithuania in 1904. They were the parents of Ruth First. See Alan Wieder, *Ruth First and Joe Slovo in the War against Apartheid* (New York: Monthly Review Press, 2013), 31–35.

22. Note, Henderson to Kpaelensery, May 15, 1936, RGASPI 495.14.345.

23. Filatova and Davidson, *Hidden Thread,* 116–18.

24. She received the nickname "Betty Red Kerchief" because she often wore a red head wrap.

25. *Drum,* June 8, 1975.

26. Robert Edgar, interview of Hilda Johnson.

27. On Kotane, see Brian Bunting's *Moses Kotane.*

28. Filatova and Davidson, *Hidden Thread,* 102–10, and Drew, *Discordant Comrades,* 172–77.

29. Testimony of Henderson, November 23, 1935, RGASPI 495.13.141.

30. Testimony of Henderson, March 13, 1936, RGASPI 395.14.20a.

31. Testimony of Henderson, November 20, 1935, RGASPI 495.13.141.

32. Her speech appeared in *Pravda* (August 8, 1935), and the British government passed on a translation directly to South Africa's Ministry of Foreign Affairs in September (JD 1/399/13/3). See also Apollon Davidson, Irina Filatova, Valentin Gorodnov, and Sheridan Johns, eds., *South Africa and the Communist International: A Documentary History*, vol. 1 (London: Frank Cass, 2003), 18.

33. Testimony of Henderson (Josie Palmer) before Marty Commission, March 13, 1936, RGASPI 493.14.349, 86.

34. Testimony of Henderson.

35. Testimony of Henderson, November 22, 1935, RGASPI 495.64.191.

36. Drew, *Discordant Comrades,* 175–76.

37. Davidson et al., *South Africa,* 10. Both Zusmanovich and Ivan Potekhin were forced to leave KUTV because they had invited George Sacks, a Cape Town journalist who was wrongly perceived to be a Trotskyite, to lecture there. KUTV was shut down in 1938.

38. Karl Schlogel, *Moscow 1937* (Cambridge: Polity, 2012), 1.

39. William Chase, *Enemies within the Gates?: The Comintern and the Stalinist Repression, 1934–1939* (New Haven, CT: Yale University Press, 2001), 7.

40. Schlogel, *Moscow 1937,* 401. See also Stephen Kotkin, *Stalin: Waiting for Hitler, 1929–1941* (New York: Penguin, 2017) and Oleg Khlevniuk, *Stalin: New Biography of a Dictator* (New Haven, CT: Yale University Press, 2015).

41. Filatova and Davidson, *Hidden Thread,* 106. Gillian Slovo's *Every Secret Thing: My Family, My Country* (London: Virago, 1997), 272–77, imputed that Josie was responsible for Bach's fate because of her testimony before the Marty Commission. Slovo reported on her grandmother Tilly going to the

Soviet Union, where she was given a free holiday at a sanatorium in Yalta because of her husband's generosity to the CPSA. At the sanatorium, she had had an affair with Bach. When referring to the speech Josie had delivered at the Seventh Congress, Slovo noted that when the Marty Commission held its hearings, it had asked her about the speech—and that she claimed that she read from a text that Bach prepared. Without any firm evidence, Slovo then drew the conclusion that Josie was somehow implicated in Bach's eventual demise: "Which meant that the woman whom Tilly had helped to get to Moscow had blown the whistle on Tilly's lover" (276).

42. Henderson to Kpaelensery, May 15, 1936.

43. Acting Secretary for the Interior to Commissioner for Immigration and Asiatic Affairs, September, 10 1936, KAB PIO 129/8943E, NASA, Cape Archives. The report stated that she was using various aliases, including Mpama, Palmer, and Mohlomi. In her *Drum* interview of June 8, 1975, she recollected that she returned to South Africa in September rather than November.

Chapter 4: Declarations of Independence

1. Robert Edgar, interview of Hilda Johnson, Orlando East, October, 1994. Sophiatown was named after the wife of Herman Tobiansky, who had bought the land on which Sophiatown was established. The main streets were named after their children, Edith, Bertha, Gerty, Toby, and Sol.

2. Led by a hardline segregationist, Frederick Stallard, the Commission was set up in 1922 to establish government policies for dealing with urban Africans.

3. David Goodhew, *Respectability and Resistance: A History of Sophiatown* (Westport, CT: Praeger, 2004). See also Tom Lodge, *Black Politics in South Africa since 1945* (London: Longman, 1983), 94–103.

4. Steven Gish, *Alfred B. Xuma: African, American and South African* (New York: New York University Press, 2000), 58–59.

5. See Josie Mpama, "Rents Go Up in Sophiatown," *Umsebenzi,* March 10, 1933.

6. This situation continued until 1936, when rents were lowered. Goodhew, *Respectability and Resistance,* 47.

7. Mpama, "Rents Go Up in Sophiatown."

8. Shebeens were "unlicensed drinking houses selling home brewed beer." Philip Bonner and Lauren Segal, *Soweto: A History* (Johannesburg: Maskew Millen Longman, 1998), 14.

9. Christopher Ballantine, *Marabi Nights: Early South African Jazz and Vaudeville* (Johannesburg: Ravan, 1993), 53.

10. Meschack Mabogoane, "Tsotsitaal," in *Kortboy: A Sophiatown Legacy,* ed. Derrick Thema (Cape Town: Kwela Books, 1999), 98–104. Tsotsitaal is a language whose base is Afrikaans and a mix of English and African languages. On tsotsis, see Clive Glaser, *Bo-Tsotsi: The Youth Gangs of Soweto, 1935–1976* (Portsmouth, NH: Heinemann, 2000), 47–70.

11. Don Mattera, *Memory Is the Weapon* (Johannesburg: Ravan, 1987), 76.

12. Dugmore Boetie, *Familiarity Is the Kingdom of the Lost* (New York: Four Walls Eight Windows, 1969), 18–19.

13. Jameson Coka, "How African Women Make Their Living," *Capitol Plaindealer,* November 22, 1936. Coka was a CPSA member until he was expelled in 1935. He wrote often in African newspapers, but he also found an outlet for his pieces through Claude Barnett's Associated Negro Press, which distributed articles through the African American press.

14. Robert Edgar, interview of Carol Matsie, Mofolo Central, February 7, 1995.

15. J. N. Spence, Deputy Commissioner, SAP, Witwatersrand Division, to Commissioner, SAP, Pretoria, December 18, 1936, Native Affairs (NTS) 7670/86/332/1.

16. *Umsebenzi,* May 29, 1937; *Bantu World,* January 23, 1937.

17. *Bantu World,* September 30, 1937.

18. Report on Party, n.d., RGASPI 395.64 or 14.149.

19. Wolfson, Report on South Africa, October 1937, RGASP 495.14.355.

20. Josie Mpama, "Educating Our Bantu Women," *Mochochonono,* November 22, 1933.

21. Testimony of Henderson, March 19, 1936, RGASPI 495.64.14.

22. Testimony of Henderson. Josie had previously published one article, "Rents Go Up in Sophiatown," *Umsebenzi*, November 10, 1933.

23. As an alternative, she had contributed articles to *Mochochono* (November 22, 1933) and a student magazine. I have not been able to identify the student magazine.

24. Testimony of Henderson, November 28, 1935, RGASPI 495.64.141.

25. Report on South Africa Question October 1937, RGASPI 495.14.355.

26. Robert Edgar, interview of Ray Edwards, Cape Town, November 13, 1994.

27. Jack and Ray Simons Papers, University of Cape Town Library, Manuscripts Division, BC 1081.013.1.

28. Jack and Ray Simons Papers, BC 1081.013.1.

29. In an interview that Tony Karon conducted four decades later with party members Issy and Ann Hayman, they confirmed the different lives that black and white members lived outside party meetings: "We would sit in a meeting, and the blacks went one way, we went the other way. We didn't walk out in the streets together. There was no such thing as inviting them over to our houses. We didn't think of that. We thought of the important things—we thought of the revolution. But the human aspect—you can't win people with theory only—that we sort of missed out." Tony Karon, interview with Issy and Ann Hayman, November 22, 1988, Historical Papers Research Archive, Witwatersrand University, AL 259(f).

30. On Seme, see Bongani Ngqulunga, *The Man Who Founded the ANC: A Biography of Pixley ka Isaka Seme* (Cape Town: Penguin Random House, 2017).

31. National Conference of the Communist Party of South Africa, September 1936, RGASPI 495.14.343.

32. J. N. Spence, Deputy Commissioner, SAP, Witwatersrand Division, to Commissioner, SAP, Pretoria, December 18, 1936, NTS 7670/86/332/1.

33. Deputy Commissioner, Witwatersrand Division, SAP, to Commissioner, SAP, Pretoria, January 14, 1937, NTS 7670 86/332/1.

34. The NEUF was closely aligned with the National Liberation League. On both organizations, see Gavin Lewis, *Between
the Wire and the Wall: A History of South African "Coloured"
Politics* (Cape Town: David Philip, 1987), 179–98.

35. *Sun* (Cape Town), June 9, 1939. District Six was a multiracial area near downtown Cape Town.

36. *Sun,* April 28, 1939.

37. *Drum,* June 8, 1975.

38. Baruch Hirson, *Yours for the Union: Class and Community Struggles in South Africa, 1930–1947* (Johannesburg:
Witwatersrand University Press, 1990), 136–47; Philip Bonner
and Noor Nieftagodien, *Alexandra: A History* (Johannesburg:
Witwatersrand University Press, 2008).

39. *Rand Daily Mail,* May 10, 1939.

40. Not all Alexandra activists welcomed Josie's involvement
in the township's affairs. Dan Koza, a trade unionist, slated her
as an outsider who had no business intruding into Alexandra
(*Rand Daily Mail,* May 15, 1939). John Nauright suggests the
rift between the two may have been because Palmer could have
been championing Alexandra tenants over standholders, but
there is no concrete evidence to support this. A more likely
explanation for Koza's antipathy is that he had Trotskyite lean-
ings that fueled his resentment toward the communist Palmer
operating on his turf. On Koza, see Baruch Hirson, "Daniel
Koza: A Working Class Leader," in *A History of the Left in South
Africa: Writings of Baruch Hirson,* ed. Yael Hirson (London: I.
B. Taurus, 2005).

41. *Sun,* May 19, 1939.

42. On the efforts of the Johannesburg municipality to get
rid of Alexandra, see Bonner and Nieftagodien, *Alexandra,*
59–82, and John Nauright, "'I Am with You as Never Before':
Women in Urban Protest Movements, Alexandra Township,
South Africa, 1912–1945," in *Courtyards, Markets, City Streets:
Urban Women in Africa,* ed. Kathleen Sheldon (Boulder, CO:
Westview, 1996), 259–84.

43. *Transvaal Communist* 1, no. 3 (June 1939): 10–11.

44. *Chain-Breaker* (January 1940); Deputy Commissioner,
Witwatersrand Division, South African Police, to Commis-

sioner, South African Police, Pretoria, December 12, 1939, NTS7670 83/332(b). Josie was secretary of the Youth Peace League, which published the newspaper *Chain-Breaker*. For how the South African left dealt with World War II, see Allison Drew, *Discordant Comrades: Identities and Loyalties on the South African Left* (Burlington, VT: Ashgate, 2000), 226–38.

45. This observation comes from an interview Peter Delius conducted with Rusty Bernstein on June 18, 1990. I thank Gabriele Mohale of the Historical Papers Research and Archive at Witwatersrand University for sharing it with me.

46. Gish, *Alfred B. Xuma,* 127, 136–38; Peter Walshe, *The Rise of African Nationalism in South Africa: The African National Congress, 1912–1952* (Berkeley: University of California Press, 1971), 312–14.

47. *Guardian,* June 14, 1943.

48. *Guardian,* April 6, 1944.

49. Elinor Sisulu, *Walter and Albertina Sisulu: In Our Lifetime* (Cape Town: David Philip, 2002), 91.

50. *Guardian,* June 1, 1944.

51. *Inkululeko,* June 23, 1945.

52. Josie Mpama, "The Anti-Pass Campaign," *Inkululeko,* March 24, 1945.

53. Sisulu, *Walter and Albertina Sisulu.* Besides Sisulu, Youth League leaders included Nelson Mandela, Oliver Tambo, Anton Lembede, and A. P. Mda. On the Youth League, see Gail Gerhart, *Black Power in South Africa: The Evolution of an Ideology* (Berkeley: University of California Press, 1978); Robert Edgar and Luyanda ka Msumza, eds., *Freedom in Our Lifetime: The Collected Writings of Anton Muziwakhe Lembede* (Athens: Ohio University Press, 1996); and Robert Edgar and Luyanda ka Msumza, eds., *Africa's Cause Must Triumph: The Collected Writings of A. P. Mda* (Cape Town: HSRC Press, 2018).

54. For discussions of the debates on black women and motherism, see Meghan Healy-Clancy, "Women and the Problem of Family in Early African Nationalist History and Historiography," *South African Historical Journal* 64, no. 3 (2012): 453–60, and Nomboniso Gasa, "Let Them Build More Gaols,"

and "Feminisms, Motherisms, Patriarchies and Women's Voices in the 1950s," in *Women in South African History: They Remove Boulders and Cross Rivers,* ed. Nomboniso Gasa (Cape Town: HSRC Press, 2007), 129–152, 207–232.

55. Josie Mpama, "Educating Our Bantu Women," *Mochochonono,* November 22, 1933.

56. Mpama.

57. Shireen Hassim, *The ANC Women's League: Sex, Gender and Politics* (Athens: Ohio University Press, 2014).

58. Wolfson, Report on South African Question, October 1937, RGAPSI 495.14.355.

59. Josie Mpama, "An Appeal to African Women to Join the Struggle against Oppressive Laws," *South African Worker,* January 30, 1937.

60. Natasha Erlank, "Gender and Masculinity in South African Nationalist Discourse," *Feminist Studies* 29, no. 3 (2003): 653–72.

61. Mpama, "An Appeal to African Women."

62. Josie Mpama, "African Women Must Be Organised: We Are Prepared to Move," *South African Worker,* June 26, 1937.

63. Gasa, *Women in South African History,* 147.

64. Healy-Clancy, "Women and the Problem of Family," 464–70.

65. *Bantu World,* January 4, 1941.

66. *Guardian,* April 24, 1947, cited in Cherryl Walker, *Women and Resistance in South Africa* (New York: Monthly Review Press, 1991), 102. The reference to "women of other nations" referred to the Women's International Democratic Federation, an association of socialist women that held a conference in Prague in 1947. One of the delegates was a South African communist, Hilda Watts. Josie was delegated to attend the conference, but the South African government turned down her application for a passport.

67. Maggie Resha, *Mangoana Tsoara Thipa ka Bohaleng: My Life in the Struggle* (Johannesburg: Congress of South African Writers, 1991), 159.

68. Maxine Molyneux, "Analysing Women's Movements," *Development and Change* 29, no. 1 (1998): 219–45, cited in

Women's Organizations and Democracy in South Africa, ed. Shireen Hassim (Madison: University of Wisconsin Press, 2006), 5.

69. Josie Mpama, "The Broadway to Heaven," *Inkululeko,* March 24, 1945.

70. Letter of Wolfson to Comrade, April 15, 1937, RGASPI 495.14.350; NTS 2931 17/304.

71. Mpama, "African Women Must Be Organised."

72. Paul La Hausse, *Brewers, Beerhalls and Boycotts: A History of Liquor in South Africa* (Johannesburg: Ravan, 1988), and Philip Bonner, "'Desirable or Undesirable Basotho Women': Liquor, Prostitution and the Migration of Basotho Women to the Rand, 1920–1945," in *Women and Gender in Southern Africa to 1945,* ed. Cherryl Walker (London: James Currey, 1990), 221–50.

73. Report on Party, n.d., RGASPI 495.64.149. A stokvel is a club of women who contribute money to a common fund for regularly hosting parties, the profits from which are distributed to members.

74. NTS 7032 31/322(6), part 2.

75. Skokiaan is a potent brew made from porridge, bread, sugar, and corn syrup. The women who brewed it were known as "skokiaan queens."

Chapter 5: Apartheid

1. Colin Bundy, *Nelson Mandela* (Stroud: History Press, 2015), 48.

2. Christopher Merritt, *A Culture of Censorship: Censorship, Secrecy and Intellectual Repression in South Africa* (Cape Town: David Philip, 1994). Before the act was passed, the CPSA executive dissolved the party, on June 20, 1950.

3. Vernon Berrange was a member of the Communist Party.

4. Letter, liquidator to Berrange and Wasserzug, Johannesburg, February 7, 1951. This letter is in Josie Mpama's banning file, which I was permitted to see at the Department of Justice in 1995. Subsequently all banning files have been transferred to the National Archives in Pretoria. Only family

members are allowed to request the files of formerly banned individuals.

5. One listed person appealed to the secretary for justice, asking him to "consult your police record regarding my past and present activities." Once the investigation was conducted, the liquidator decided not to list him "because he was a paid informer." I have decided not to make this person's name known.

6. Letter included in Josie Mpama's banning file.

7. Letter included in Josie Mpama's banning file.

8. African women did not have to carry passes in the Orange Free State after they led protests in that province in 1913. The ban on African women carrying passes was extended nationally in the early 1920s.

9. Maggie Resha, *Mangoana Tsoara Thipa ka Bohaleng: My Life in the Struggle* (Johannesburg: Congress of South African Writers, 1991).

10. *Inkululeko,* May 1950.

11. Information included in Josie Mpama's banning file.

12. Information included in Josie Mpama's banning file.

13. Deborah Posel, *The Making of Apartheid, 1948–1961: Conflict and Compromise* (Oxford: Clarendon Press, 1991), 207.

14. Iris Berger, "African Women's Movements in the Twentieth Century: A Hidden History," *African Studies Review* 57, no. 3 (December 2014): 13.

15. Jane Barrett, Aneene Dawber, Barbara Klugman, Ingrid Obery, Jennifer Shindler, and Joanne Yawitch, *Vukani Makhosikazi: South African Women Speak* (London: Catholic Institute for International Relations, 1985), 238.

16. Barrett et al., 240.

17. Interview, Ray Alexander, Cape Town, May 31, 1995.

18. Cherryl Walker, *Women and Resistance in South Africa* (New York: Monthly Review Press, 1991), 170.

19. Robert Edgar, interview with Belinda Palmer, Braamfontein, August 7, 1998.

20. The Freedom Charter contained the core principles and policies of the Congress Alliance, which consisted of the

ANC and its allies—the South African Indian Congress, the Coloured People's Congress, and the South African Congress of Democrats.

21. Walker, *Women and Resistance*, 182.

22. Helen Joseph, *Side by Side: The Autobiography of Helen Joseph* (New York: William Morrow, 1986), 44–45.

23. Joseph, 183.

24. Julia Wells, *We Now Demand! The History of Women's Resistance to Pass Laws in South Africa* (Johannesburg: Witwatersrand University Press, 1993), 109.

25. Wells, 110–13, and Walker, *Women and Resistance*, 194–97.

26. *New Age,* January 6, 1956. A provision of the Suppression of Communism Act, banning orders could impose a range of restrictions on individuals such as preventing them from attending meetings, writing anything for publication, being quoted in magazines and newspapers, and leaving one's home or an area. For more details, see Roger Omond, *The Apartheid Handbook: A Guide to South Africa's Everyday Racial Policies,* 2nd ed. (New York: Penguin, 1986), 193–200. According to the South African Institute of Race Relations, the government issued banning orders to 1,240 persons from 1950 to 1974. John Dugard, *Human Rights and the South African Legal Order* (Princeton, NJ: Princeton University Press, 1974), 139.

27. Brian Bunting, *The Rise of the South African Reich* (Harmondsworth, UK: Penguin, 1964), 165. The government borrowed the language of "feelings of hostility" directly from the Riotous Assemblies Act of 1930.

28. Trevor Huddleston, *Naught for Your Comfort* (Johannesburg: Hardingham & Donaldson, 1956), 144.

29. Josie Palmer to Federation of South African Women, October 26, 1955, FEDSAW correspondence, RD 1137/Ba3, Historical Papers Research Archive, Witwatersrand University.

30. Ngoyi grew up in a rural area where her mother, like Josie, laundered clothes for a white family. When they delivered the clothes to the white home, they were expected to go to the kitchen door at the back. Ngoyi said, "In the white man's

house, the dog would jump on the missis and go on her bed or anywhere in the house, but my mother's baby, a human being, could not be fed inside the house. That began to make me bitter." In Johannesburg, Ngoyi found work as a seamstress and then joined the Garment Workers' Union. Anthony Sampson, *The Treason Cage: The Opposition on Trial in South Africa* (London: Heinemann, 1958), 140.

31. Richard Elphick, *The Equality of Believers: Protestant Missionaries and the Racial Politics of South Africa* (Charlottesville: University of Virginia Press, 2012), 288.

32. Robert Edgar, interview with Belinda Palmer, August 7, 1998. The Anglican hierarchy split over how best to respond to Bantu Education. See Michael Worsnip, *Between the Two Fires: The Anglican Church and Apartheid, 1948–1957* (Pietermaritzburg: University of Natal Press, 1991).

33. Vusi Khumalo, interview with Lorraine Johnson, Orlando East, July 23, 2013.

34. On March 21, the Pan Africanist Congress, the ANC's main rival, launched a nationwide campaign against pass laws. At Sharpeville, South African police fired on protesters, killing sixty-nine.

35. See the website for Constitution Hill at www .constitutionhill.org.za/sites/site-womens-jail.

Chapter 6: Comrades and Christians

1. "SOWETO" was a bureaucratic acronym for South West Township.

2. I mention this because I have anecdotal evidence of a subculture of families living in Soweto whose home language is Afrikaans. They are probably the descendants of Oorlams who migrated to Soweto from small towns and rural areas in the Transvaal Province. The topic is worthy of a research project.

3. Robin Kelley, *Hammer and Hoe: Alabama Communists during the Great Depression* (Chapel Hill: University of North Carolina Press, 1990), 196.

4. Charles Villa-Vicencio, *The Spirit of Hope: Conversations on Religion, Politics and Values* (Johannesburg: Skotaville Publishers, 1994), 54.

5. Villa-Vicencio, 120.

6. Mia Brandel-Syrier, *Black Woman in Search of God* (London: Lutterworth Press, 1962), 139. Brandel-Syrier did not identify this person, and I have not located her field notes. *Manyano* members were known for their distinctive uniforms and for their prayer and devotion to their faith. For urban African women living in a disempowering environment, manyanos offered a spiritual home as well as a structured support system, a set of rules that governed their behavior, a hierarchy of authority, and an independent space where they controlled their own affairs and asserted their leadership.

7. Nelson Mandela, *Long Walk to Freedom* (Randburg: Macdonald Purnell, 1994), 174.

8. Villa-Vicencio, *Spirit of Hope,* 118. Later in the 1960s, Hani became highly critical of the church and rejected his religious beliefs.

9. Kelley, *Hammer and Hoe,* 108.

10. Villa-Vicencio, *Spirit of Hope,* 253.

11. A select number of CPSA members were invited to join the underground wing. See Raymond Suttner, *The ANC Underground in South Africa to 1976: A Social and Historical Study* (Auckland Park: Jacana Media, 2007), 39–49.

12. Philip Bonner and Lauren Segal, *Soweto: A History* (Johannesburg: Maskew Millen Longman, 1998).

13. Her half sister Vesta Smith (1922–2013), who lived in Noordgesig, was also a political activist. An ANC member, she participated in the Congress of the People at Kliptown in 1955 and the women's march on the Union buildings in 1956. She was detained during the 1976 Soweto Uprising, as well as in 1980 and 1986, and was a founding member of the United Democratic Front. See her profile at www.sahistory.org.za /people/vesta-smith.

14. "Comfort in Moscow for Josie," *Drum,* June 8, 1975.

15. Iris Berger, "African Women's Movements in the Twentieth Century: A Hidden History," *African Studies Review* 57, no. 3 (2014): 9.

16. Robert Edgar, telephone interview with Virginia Palmer.

17. Robert Edgar, interview with Maggie Nkwe, Klerksdorp, July 15, 2004. Eventually Maggie qualified as a nurse at Baragwanath Hospital and served there from 1959 to 1978. David Nkwe became an Anglican priest at St. Paul's in Jabavu before he was selected as bishop of Klerksdorp.

18. Robert Edgar, interview, Mzimhlophe Township, June 21, 1998, with Ms. H. M. Lichaba, Mrs. S. Matlejoane, Ms. G. Skele, and Mrs. N. Lichaba.

19. An interesting observation about nonwhite members of the Communist Party is that on issues of language and culture, they were part and parcel of their communities. Flag Boshielo trained as an herbalist, Dr. Yusuf Dadoo went on the hajj to Mecca, and Edwin Mofutsanyana organized circumcision schools for teen-aged boys when he was in exile in Lesotho.

20. Robert Edgar, interview with Lorraine Johnson, Mzimhlophe.

21. Robert Edgar, interview with Belinda Palmer, Mzimhlophe.

22. Bonner and Segal, *Soweto*, 78–99.

23. In exile, Lorraine lived in Swaziland and eventually served with Umkhonto we Sizwe in Mozambique and Angola. She later moved to Canada, where she lived until the early 1990s, when she returned to South Africa. Interview, Lorraine Johnson by Vusi Khumalo, July 23, 2013. I thank Vusi Kumalo for conducting this interview.

24. "ANC Veteran Palmer Dies," *Post* (Johannesburg), December 4, 1979.

25. Walter Sisulu to Babsie (Carol) Matsie, March 8, 1980. I thank Carol Matsie for sharing this letter with me. When I accompanied Sisulu to Edwin Mofutsanyana's funeral in early 1995, he warmly greeted Hilda Johnson, Edwin's and Josie's daughter, and told her that she should not be intimidated by his fame and should feel free to reach out to him and his wife Albertina.

Conclusion: Get Up and Get Moving

1. *Drum,* June 8, 1975.

Appendix: Josie Mpama/Palmer on Gender and Politics

1. Mpama was responding to a letter from Caswell Molapo, "Educating Our Bantu Women," that appeared in the September 27, 1933, issue of *Mochochonono.* Molapo advocated that women should be encouraged to do more than domestic chores and play a "part in social, educational, political, and religious fields." He argued that the idea that women are inferior to men was a distortion of Christian teaching. Jesus Christ, he said, preached that there should be no distinction between men and women. Hence, women should be given the same educational opportunities as men. He concluded his letter with "May there the Bantu awaken and educate their daughters and sisters."

Interviews

Peter Delius
   Rusty Bernstein, June 18, 1990.

Robert Edgar
   Ray Alexander, Cape Town, May 31, 1995.
   Ray Edwards, Cape Town, November 13, 1994.
   Hilda Johnson, Orlando East, October 1994.
   Mrs. H. M. Lichaba, Ms. G. Skele, Mrs. S. Matle-
      joane, and Mrs. N. Lichaba, Mzimhlophe, June
      21, 1998.
   Esme Matshikiza, Cape Town, February 16, 1995.
   Carol Matsie, Mofolo Central, February 7, 1995.
   Edwin Mofutsanyana, Roma, Lesotho, July 1980.
   Maggie Nkwe, Klerksdorp, July 15, 2004.
   Belinda Palmer, Braamfontein, August 7, 1998.
   Virginia Palmer, Durban, October 15, 2014.
   Vesta Smith, Noordgesig, March 6, 1995.

Tony Karen
   Issy and Ann Hayman, November 22, 1988.

Vusi Khumalo
   Lorraine Johnson, July 23, 2013.

Julia Wells
   Josie Mpama/Palmer, Mzimhlophe, October 1977.

Bibliography

Adi, Hakim. "The Communist International and Black Libera-
    tion in the Interwar Years." In *From Toussaint to Tupac:
    The Black International since the Age of Revolution,* ed-
    ited by Michael West, William Martin, and Fanon Che
    Wilkins, 155–75. Chapel Hill: University of North Caro-
    lina Press, 2009.

Ballantine, Christopher. *Marabi Nights: Early South African
    Jazz and Vaudeville.* Johannesburg: Ravan, 1993.

Barrett, Jane, Aneene Dawber, Barbara Klugman, Ingrid Obery,
    Jennifer Shindler, and Joanne Yawitch. *Vukani Mak-
    hosikazi: South African Women Speak.* London: Catholic
    Institute for International Relations, 1985.

Berger, Iris. "African Women's Movements in the Twentieth
    Century: A Hidden History." *African Studies Review* 57,
    no. 3 (2014): 1–19.

———. *Threads of Solidarity: Women in South African Indus-
    try.* Bloomington: Indiana University Press, 1992.

Boetie, Dugmore. *Familiarity Is the Kingdom of the Lost.* New
    York: Four Walls Eight Windows, 1969.

Bonner, Philip. "'Desirable or Undesirable Basotho Women':
    Liquor, Prostitution and the Migration of Basotho
    Women to the Rand, 1920–1945." In *Women and Gen-
    der in Southern Africa to 1945,* edited by Cherryl Walker,
    221–50. London: James Currey, 1990.

Bonner, Philip, and Noor Nieftagodien. *Alexandra: A History.*
    Johannesburg: Witwatersrand University Press, 2008.

Bonner, Philip, and Lauren Segal. *Soweto: A History.* Johannes-
    burg: Maskew Millen Longman, 1998.

Brandel-Syrier, Mia. *Black Women in Search of God*. London: Lutterssworth, 1962.

Bundy, Colin. *Nelson Mandela*. Stroud: History Press, 2015.

Bunting, Brian. *Moses Kotane: A South African Revolutionary; A Political Biography*. London: Inkululeko Publications, 1975.

———. *The Rise of the South African Reich*. Harmondsworth, UK: Penguin, 1964.

Chanock, Martin. *The Making of South African Legal Culture, 1902–1936: Fear, Power and Prejudice*. Cambridge: Cambridge University Press, 2001.

Chase, William. *Enemies within the Gates?: The Comintern and the Stalinist Repression, 1934–1939*. New Haven, CT: Yale University Press, 2001.

"Comfort in Moscow for Josie." *Drum*, June 8, 1975.

Davidson, Apollon, Irina Filatova, Valentin Gorodnov, and Sheridan Johns, eds. *South Africa and the Communist International: A Documentary History*. 2 vols. London: Frank Cass, 2003.

Drew, Allison. *Between Empire and Revolution: A Life of Sidney Bunting, 1873–1936*. London: Pickering & Chatto, 2007.

———. *Discordant Comrades: Identities and Loyalties on the South African Left*. Burlington, VT: Ashgate, 2000.

Dugard, John. *Human Rights and the South African Legal Order*. Princeton, NJ: Princeton University Press, 1974.

Edgar, Robert. *The Making of an African Communist: Edwin Thabo Mofutsanyana and the Communist Party of South Africa, 1927–1939*. Pretoria: University of South Africa Press, 2005.

Edgar, Robert, and Luyanda ka Msumza, eds. *Africa's Cause Must Triumph: The Collected Writings of A. P. Mda*. Cape Town: HSRC Press, 2018.

———, eds. *Freedom in Our Lifetime: The Collected Writings of Anton Muziwakhe Lembede*. Athens: Ohio University Press, 1996.

Elphick, Richard. *The Equality of Believers: Protestant Missionaries and the Racial Politics on South Africa*. Charlottesville: University of Virginia Press, 2012.

Epprecht, Marc. *"This Matter of Women Is Getting Very Bad":
Gender, Development and Politics in Colonial Lesotho.*
Scottsville: University of KwaZulu Natal Press, 2000.

Erlank, Natasha. "Gender and Masculinity in South African
Nationalist Discourse." *Feminist Studies* 29, no. 3 (2003):
653–72.

Filatova, Irina, and Apollon Davidson. *The Hidden Thread:
Russia and South Africa in the Soviet Era.* Johannesburg:
Jonathan Ball, 2013.

Gasa, Nomboniso, ed. *Women in South African History: They
Remove Boulders and Cross Rivers.* Cape Town: HSRC
Press, 2007.

Gerhart, Gail. *Black Power in South Africa: The Evolution of an
Ideology.* Berkeley: University of California Press, 1978.

Gish, Steven. *Alfred B. Xuma: African, American, South African.* New York: New York University Press, 2000.

Glaser, Clive. *Bo-Tsotsi: The Youth Gangs of Soweto, 1935–1976.*
Portsmouth, NH: Heinemann, 2000.

Goodhew, David. *Respectability and Resistance: A History of
Sophiatown.* Westport, CT: Praeger, 2004.

Hassim, Shireen. *The ANC Women's League: Sex, Gender and
Politics.* Athens: Ohio University Press, 2014.

———. *Women's Organization and Democracy in South Africa.* Madison: University of Wisconsin Press, 2006.

Healy-Clancy, Meghan. "Women and the Problem of Family
in Early African Nationalist History and Historiography."
South African Historical Journal 64, no. 3 (2012): 450–71.

Hirson, Baruch. "Daniel Koza: A Working-Class Leader." In *A
History of the Left in South Africa: Writings of Baruch Hirson,* edited by Yael Hirson, 180–206. London: I. B. Taurus,
2005.

———. *Yours for the Union: Class and Community Struggles in
South Africa, 1930–1947.* Johannesburg: Witwatersrand
University Press, 1990.

Huddleston, Trevor. *Naught for Your Comfort.* Johannesburg:
Hardingham & Donaldson, 1956.

Jaffer, Zubeida. *Beauty of the Heart: The Life and Times of Charlotte Manye Maxeke.* Bloemfontein: Sun Media, 2016.

Joseph, Helen. *Side by Side: The Autobiography of Helen Joseph.* New York: William Morrow, 1986.

Keller, Emma Gilboy. *Lady: The Life and Times of Winnie Mandela.* London: Vintage, 1994.

Kelley, Robin. *Hammer and Hoe: Alabama Communists during the Great Depression.* Chapel Hill: University of North Carolina Press, 1990.

Khlevniuk, Oleg. *Stalin: New Biography of a Dictator.* New Haven, CT: Yale University Press, 2015.

Kotkin, Stephen. *Stalin: Waiting for Hitler, 1929–1941.* New York: Penguin, 2017.

Kuzwayo, Ellen. *Call Me Woman.* Johannesburg: Ravan, 1995.

La Hausse, Paul. *Brewers, Beerhalls and Boycotts: A History of Liquor in South Africa.* Johannesburg: Ravan, 1988.

Lawrance, Benjamin N., Emily Lynn Osborn, and Richard L. Roberts, eds. *Intermediaries, Interpreters, and Clerks: African Employees in the Making of Colonial Africa.* Madison: University of Wisconsin Press, 2006.

Lewis, Gavin. *Between the Wire and the Wall: A History of South African "Coloured" Politics.* Cape Town: David Philip, 1987.

Lodge, Tom. *Black Politics in South Africa since 1945.* London: Longman, 1983.

Mabogoane, Meschack. "Tsotsitaal." In *Kortboy: A Sophiatown Legacy,* edited by Derrick Thema, 98–104. Cape Town: Kwela Books, 1999.

Mandela, Nelson. *Long Walk to Freedom.* Randburg: Macdonald Purnell, 1994.

Mashinini, Emma. *Strikes Have Followed Me All My Life: A South African Autobiography.* New York: Routledge, 1991.

Mattera, Don. *Memory Is the Weapon.* Johannesburg: Ravan, 1987.

Maylam, Paul. "The Rise and Decline of Urban Apartheid in South Africa." *African Affairs* 89, no. 354 (1990): 57–84.

McClellan, Woodford. "Africans and Black Americans in the Comintern Schools, 1925–1934." *International Journal of African Historical Studies* 26, no. 2 (1993): 371–90.

———. "Black Hajj to 'Red Mecca': Africans and Afro-Americans at KUTV, 1925–1938." In *Africa in Russia,*

Russia in Africa: Three Centuries of Encounters, edited by Maxim Matusevich, 61–84. Trenton, NJ: Africa World Press, 2007.

Merritt, Christopher. *A Culture of Censorship: Censorship, Secrecy and Intellectual Repression in South Africa.* Cape Town: David Philip, 1994.

Mpama, Josie. "Autobiography of J. Mpama [1936]." In *South Africa and the Communist International: A Documentary History,* vol. 2. Edited by Apollon Davidson, Irina Filatova, Valentin Gorodnov, and Sheridan Johns, 160–70. London: Frank Cass, 2003.

Nauright, John. "'I Am with You as Never Before': Women in Urban Protest Movements, Alexandra Township, South Africa, 1912–1945." In *Courtyards, Markets, City Streets: Urban Women in Africa,* edited by Kathleen Sheldon, 259–83. Boulder, CO: Westview, 1996.

Ngqulunga, Bongani. *The Man Who Founded the ANC: A Biography of Pixley ka Isaka Seme.* Cape Town: Penguin Random House, 2017.

Odendaal, Andre. *The Founders: The Origins of the African National Congress and the Struggle for Democracy in South Africa.* Lexington: University Press of Kentucky, 2013.

Omond, Roger. *The Apartheid Handbook: A Guide to South Africa's Everyday Racial Policies.* 2nd ed. New York: Penguin, 1986.

Plaatje, Solomon. "The Essential Interpreter." In *Sol Plaatje: Selected Writings,* edited by Brian Willan, 50–60. Athens: Ohio University Press, 1997.

Plaut, Martin. *Promise and Despair: The First Struggle for a Non-Racial South Africa.* Athens: Ohio University Press, 2017.

Posel, Deborah. *The Making of Apartheid, 1948–1961: Conflict and Compromise.* Oxford: Clarendon Press, 1991.

Resha, Maggie. *Mangoana Tsoara Thipa ka Bohaleng: My Life in the Struggle.* Johannesburg: Congress of South African Writers, 1991.

Ross, Robert, Anne Mager, and Bill Nasson, eds. *The Cambridge History of South Africa.* Vol. 2. Cambridge: Cambridge University Press, 2011.

Roth, Mia. *The Communist Party in South Africa: Racism, Eurocentricity and Moscow, 1921–1950*. Johannesburg: Partridge Africa, 2016.

———. "Josie Mpama: The Contribution of a Largely Forgotten Figure in the South African Liberation Struggle." *Kleio* 28 (1996): 120–36.

Sampson, Anthony. *The Treason Cage: The Opposition on Trial in South Africa*. London: Heinemann, 1958.

Scanlon, Helen. *Representation and Reality: Portraits of Women's Lives in the Western Cape, 1948–1972*. Cape Town: HSRC Press, 2007.

Schlogel, Karl. *Moscow 1937*. Cambridge: Polity, 2012.

Simons, Jack, and Ray Simons. *Class and Colour in South Africa, 1850–1950*. London: Penguin, 1969.

Simons, Ray Alexander. *All My Life and All My Strength*. Edited by Raymond Suttner. Johannesburg: STE Publishers, 2004.

Sisulu, Elinor. *Walter and Albertina Sisulu: In Our Lifetime*. Cape Town: David Philip, 2002.

Skota, T. D. Mweli. *The African Yearly Register, Being an Illustrated National Biographical Dictionary (Who's Who) of Black Folks in Africa*. Johannesburg: Esson (printer), 1931.

Slovo, Gillian. *Every Secret Thing: My Family, My Country*. London: Virgo, 1997.

Suttner, Raymond. *The ANC Underground in South Africa to 1976: A Social and Historical Study*. Auckland Park: Jacana Media, 2007.

van Rensburg, Fanie Jansen. "Protest by Potchefstroom Native Location's Residents against Dominance, 1904 to 1950." *Historia* 57, no. 1 (2012): 23–41.

Villa-Vicencio, Charles. *The Spirit of Hope: Conversations on Religion, Politics and Values*. Johannesburg: Skotaville Publishers, 1994.

Walker, Cherryl. *Women and Resistance in South Africa*. New York: Monthly Review Press, 1991.

Walshe, Peter. *The Rise of African Nationalism in South Africa: The African National Congress, 1912–1952*. Berkeley: University of California Press, 1971.

Wells, Julia. "'The Day the Town Stood Still': Women in Resistance in Potchefstroom, 1912–1930." In *Town and Countryside in the Transvaal: Capitalist Penetration and Popular Response,* edited by Belinda Bozzoli, 269–307. Johannesburg: Ravan, 1983.

———. *We Now Demand! The History of Women's Resistance to Pass Laws in South Africa.* Johannesburg: Witwatersrand University Press, 1993.

Wieder, Alan. *Ruth First and Joe Slovo in the War against Apartheid.* New York: Monthly Review Press, 2013.

Willan, Brian. *Sol Plaatje: A Life of Solomon Tshekiso Plaatje, 1876–1932.* Charlottesville: University of Virginia Press, 2019.

Worsnip, Michael. *Between the Two Fires: The Anglican Church and Apartheid, 1948–1957.* Pietermaritzburg: University of Natal Press, 1991.

Index